Iridescent Passages

*One Family's Story of Death and
Despair and the Miracle of Prayer*

Larry, Gayle, and Craig Powell

ARCHWAY
PUBLISHING

Archway Publishing books may be ordered through booksellers or by contacting:

Archway Publishing
1663 Liberty Drive
Bloomington, IN 47403
www.archwaypublishing.com
1 (888) 242-5904

Cover image: Larry Powell

ISBN: 978-1-4808-3201-5 (sc)
ISBN: 978-1-4808-3202-2 (hc)
ISBN: 978-1-4808-3203-9 (e)

Library of Congress Control Number: 2016943578

Print information available on the last page.

Archway Publishing rev. date: 06/08/2016

Contents

Foreword

When I was first asked if I would be willing to contribute a small introduction to this book, I was honored and struck by the privilege being offered to me. I also immediately understood that I would never be able to do justice in a few words to the depth of power and majesty involved with the healing and resurrection of a human being or a family.

Introductions being in order, my name is Don L. I prefer not to use my last name, as I am a member of a twelve-step program where anonymity is a foundation of our very society. The spirit of anonymity also helps guard me individually from the grandiose idea that I had anything of real significance to do with the miracle at hand within the Powell family. I am witness—nothing more, nothing less—to the healing power of God and the miracle that has come to visit this family.

I understand a little bit about this power, as all the good in my life is directly attributable to my introduction to God and sobriety more than twenty-four years ago. My own personal story is testament to this power, which can take a young man who is broken in every way that a human being can be broken—hopelessly in dept, unemployed and unemployable, disassociated from society, and estranged from his family—to the life of peace and contentment that I enjoy today.

I look at what I am today—approaching twenty years in a loving marriage, successful in business, responsible as a citizen, accountable in all the ways that you would want a family member to be—and think, *You can't get here from there.* But in reality, you can. I believe there is a power available to every man, woman, and child. I believe this fundamental idea of God resides within all of us. This power (which my vocabulary fails to accurately describe, but seemingly comprising unlimited power, love, and guidance) is available to all who honestly seek it. One such individual on this journey of discovery was my dear friend Craig Powell.

Craig came into my life more than six years ago. It is amazing that one human being could have devastated his own life so completely under his own power, with really no adverse contributions by anyone or anything other than his own self-will. Craig arrived in recovery with the kind of résumé that is often conducive to recreating your life. It appears that the more failure you have experienced, the greater your opportunity to connect with this power that performs miracles in the lives of broken people.

This kind of profound failure seems to be relevant to and correlate with producing the most valuable commodity anyone can have when it comes to starting his or her life over, yet the sufferer often misidentifies this commodity as a deficit rather than an asset. That is understandable, because this commodity, which allows resurrection to occur, does not initially produce comforting emotions. In fact, it's quite the opposite: it keeps you up at night and doesn't allow you to sleep. Its main ingredients seem to be shame, remorse, and guilt. As negative as that sounds, there seems to be no way for a human being to start over without it. This commodity is desperation—and Craig, my dear friend, had it in abundance.

I've had the opportunity to sponsor men in recovery for most of my own twenty-four years as a member of a twelve-step program, and I would match Craig's willingness to try against that of any of the men I've had the pleasure of working with. The desperation that produced such willingness in Craig actually turned out to be the propellant that took him through the process of recovery. It allowed him to find God and recreate his life.

I think of the state Craig was in when he arrived in our twelve-step program, and I find it amazing how, although a hypodermic needle has a very small gauge, it has the ability to allow things to pass through it that are hard to comprehend. I know Craig put his parents through that needle. He put his career through that needle. He put his self-esteem, his hope, his confidence, his pride—in fact, he put all things in life that are worthwhile, that money cannot buy—through the small gauge of a hypodermic needle.

His family wanted little or nothing to do with him, and rightly so. He had taken them on the bizarre roller-coaster ride of addiction and madness. He had been anything but a father to his son, and he'd hit a low point at which the average person, if he were a betting man, would say, "This person's life is over, for all intents and purposes." Yet here we are, a short time later, and Craig has back all the things that society will tell you make for a happy life. He has the material things and the things that might seem impressive to someone looking at them from a distance.

But it's never on the outside where God does his work; it's on the inside. I've watched this man who was empty and broken become filled with love and be healed. I've watched him become a father and reunite with his son, who now lives with him. I've watched the son reunite, through the process of making amends, with a mother and father who never stopped loving him but were afraid of him. Now they vacation together, they talk regularly on the phone, and they love each other in every way that a family can love each other. I look at the miraculous work in the lives of the Powell family, and I think how very kind God has been to them. How very kind God has been to me too, and how blessed I am to have been a witness to this rebirth, this reuniting, this resurrection.

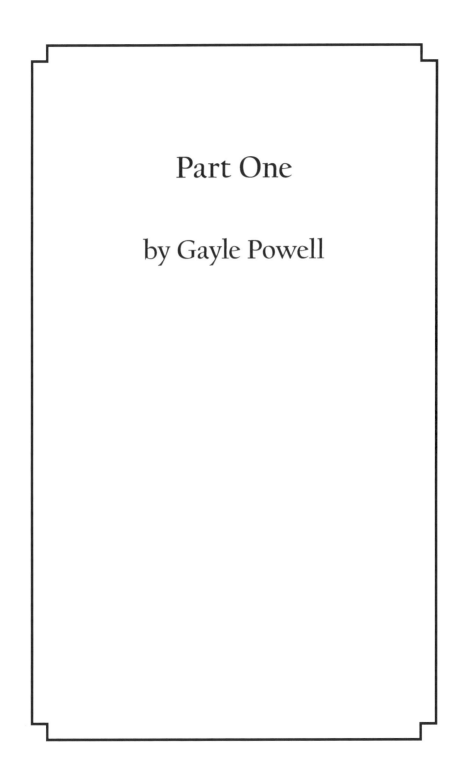

Part One

by Gayle Powell

Chapter 1:   Finding Love

We began our fifty-five-year-long journey together at the age of sixteen, when we were in high school and attended the same church.

I was not very outgoing and tended to be reserved and guarded. Larry was enthusiastic, playful, and full of energy. We had very little in common, yet we were drawn together.

For the next five years, our relationship grew and deepened. We were inseparable.

We were married on January 30, 1965, in Southern California. Our wedding was beautiful, and our hearts were filled with love and anticipation for what the future held.

We were ready to bring a new life into our lives, but soon we learned that this child would not come to us as easily as we had hoped. Larry found out that he had a low sperm count, and after he received a series of medical treatments, we were thrilled to find out that I was pregnant.

Very early on in my pregnancy, I knew deep inside my heart that this would be a very special child, but that we would have this child for only a short time. Charmaine Noel was born December 26, 1966. She was the joy of both our families, the first grandchild for both sides.

Charmaine was a very gentle little girl, sweet and well behaved. We were able to take her anywhere and do anything and never have to worry about how she would act.

For her second birthday, we invited a few neighborhood children over to celebrate. When it came time to open her gifts, Charmaine would admire each new toy and then get up and hand it to one of her guests so he or she could enjoy playing with it.

She seemed to be pleased that one of her little friends was happy playing with her birthday present.

Charmaine always had very good manners. She never missed saying please or thank you. If we told her not to touch something or to sit down or to eat, or whatever our instructions were, she would obey.

We were extremely proud, and possibly even arrogant, because we had such a good young child. We were doing everything right. We were happy; everything was in place for us. Our lives were balanced.

Chapter 2:   Looking for More Love

When Charmaine turned two, we began thinking of adding another child to our family, but soon we discovered that we would never be able to conceive again. After much thinking and after many discussions, we began the process of adopting a baby boy.

Because we lived in Southern California and were avid beachgoers, one of our requests was for a child with not very fair skin. (Sunscreen was not readily available then.)

During this period, we were also thinking that it was probably time to consider buying our own house. The Southern California housing market had really changed from the cozy communities that we had once known. Now all the affordable houses were way down in Orange County, which would mean long and stressful commute to work for Larry.

My brother, a career navy man who had spent time up in the Pacific Northwest, told us of the great way of life there. So Larry sent out résumés to several companies in the area, and when he received invitations to interview in Washington and Oregon, we decided to take a week's vacation and travel up north to see what prospects were available there.

The Seattle area was just as big as Los Angeles, with many outlying communities, and so of course that meant crowded freeways, lots of people, and long commutes to and from work. One smaller town that had good possibilities was Longview, Washington.

Larry had an interview scheduled with a printing company there, and we felt that the town might be what we were looking for. The company managers really liked Larry but told him that they would not have an opening for another year. Larry worked as a pressman in downtown Los Angeles, but the company in Longview wanted him as a sales representative. So we returned to our rented duplex in California and settled back into our familiar routines. We continued with the adoption plan and began the wait for our new baby.

One year to the date after his interview there, Larry received a phone call from the company in Longview. They were ready for him to come work for them.

In February 1970, Larry went on ahead to our new hometown to try out the sales job for a month before bringing us to join him. I stayed behind with our daughter, now three, and made all the decisions about what to pack for moving and what we really did not need anymore. Both our families were supportive of our decision, even though they were heartbroken that we were moving so far away.

One month later, Charmaine and I were on an airplane, headed for our new life in Longview. We adjusted to weather we had never known before, and to the smell of lumber mills. Larry loved his new job as a salesman, which he took on with great enthusiasm. I had never gotten my driver's license, and so Charmaine and I spent our days making our new duplex a real home.

On the weekends, the three of us would venture out on drives to explore our new and beautiful environment. We would ride up to Mount St. Helens and the surrounding lakes and forest. All the natural beauty left us awestruck.

In June, we went on our first day trip to the Washington coast, with Larry's new boss and his wife. We got a rude awakening to how much different life was in the Pacific Northwest. We'd planned for our day at the beach as we always had in Southern California, packing beach clothes, beach chairs and towels, and a sand pail and shovel. We thought we were set. We were greeted by hard, wet sand, strong winds, and very cold air and ocean water. Larry and his boss proceeded to dig for clams, while Charmaine and I spent hours with the boss's wife, sitting in the car and freezing. Yes, life in Washington was very different from what we'd known.

After a pleasant, warm summer and beautiful fall season, we looked forward to our first holiday in our new hometown.

Chapter 3: God's Second Blessing, Craig

On December 3, we received a phone call from our social worker saying the adoption agency had a two-week-old baby. The only drawback was that he had very fair skin and red hair. This was no longer an issue for us, as we were no longer living in Southern California.

On December 7, in a town north of Longview in Washington, we were introduced to a tiny red-haired baby with skin so white it looked almost translucent. We were given the little being for the day to get to know him, and that evening the social worker returned for him, telling us to take that night to decide how we felt about this baby. She said she would check with us in the morning to hear whether we felt he was suitable for our family.

When she returned to our motel and asked us how our visit had gone and what our feelings were, Charmaine said, "He is ours!" So the four of us began our three-hour drive back home with our son, whom we named Craig.

The first two and a half months went very smoothly. Craig was a sweet, calm, and happy baby. He was patient waiting for his food to arrive, and he fit right into our family. We had also added a puppy, Oliver, to our now-complete family. We had no way of knowing how drastically everything would change in an instant.

One evening when Craig had just turned three months old, we prepared him for bed as usual, changing his diaper and putting him in his cozy pj's. Then I fed him his last bottle of the day, in which he showed very little interest. Craig had always enjoyed being fed and consumed quite a lot. Not this night.

At around ten o'clock, with both our children settled in for the night, Larry and I sat down to watch TV. Suddenly the quiet was interrupted by Craig crying out loudly. Something was terribly wrong. We went to him, and I reached in his crib to pick him up, thinking a diaper pin was not secured and had stuck him. As I lay him down to check, he stopped crying: he had stopped breathing. I picked him up again quickly, and as I did, he screamed—and we knew that he was breathing again.

This pattern continued on as Larry called our doctor, who told us to get Craig to the hospital immediately. We knew we could get there faster if we drove ourselves; an ambulance would have to come out to our home and then go back to the hospital.

We noticed that Craig's color was not normal. He was not blue from lack of oxygen; he was ashen gray. As I held him in the dark on our quick drive to the hospital, he would let out a cry and then stop. Each silence meant he was not breathing.

The attendants in the ER took him, and off they went. We were left not knowing what could possibly be going on with our precious little boy.

We were sent home for the night and told to return the next day, after they had had the chance to do blood work, a spinal tap, and numerous other tests. As we walked back to our car in the dark of night, the thoughts in my head turned to the strong possibility that our time with Craig would be very short, only three months.

Upon our arrival early the next day, Craig's doctors told us that the only thing that they could find was a slightly irregular white blood count. Craig never did develop a fever. He was kept on a respirator and heart monitor and observed very closely. He remained in the hospital for three days.

We were so relieved to be bringing him home again. But he was fussy. He acted hungry, yet it was hard to get him to feed. He did not sleep that first night home except for about two hours between 5:00 and 7:00 a.m. This sleep pattern would continue for the next four years.

Craig's temperament would change as quickly as a light switch turning off and on. If he should happen to fall asleep, he was outraged when he woke up.

Through those long, difficult nights, there was no consoling him. He fought being held, rocked, or walked. As he got older, he became self-abusive. Fortunately for us, our family physician was very caring and supportive.

Chapter 4:   Our Challenge

By the time was Craig was about a year old, he would rock his crib across the room during his marathon nights. One time I walked into his room around 2:00 a.m. only to find him at his bedroom window; he had unlocked it and pushed out the screen and was halfway out the opening. When Larry bolted the crib to the middle of the wood floor, Craig's solution was to break out the mattress and frame and crawl out the bottom.

On one such night, we heard a terrible crash coming from his room, and we found his crib fallen like a house of cards. He had removed the screws and bolts! Upon reporting this to a behavioral expert, we were told that a child of Craig's age could not possibly have achieved that feat. He had no idea what this child was capable of.

As a toddler, Craig began using his teeth to bend the tines of his fork into a mangled mess. Somehow he never broke or even chipped a tooth. Physically and mentally, he was incredibly powerful.

At the age of four, while we were visiting my family on Catalina Island, Craig wrapped his arms around his grandmother's legs as she stood in the living room, and he proceeded to lift her up off the floor. As she teetered in the air, we all were saying, "Craig, put Grandma down!" He held her up there for several minutes.

He always overwhelmed us by doing things that truly seemed impossible. It was never easy to get someone to babysit him. His grandparents would not take on the challenge. My sister, Marsha, offered to watch Craig while Larry and I went out for dinner one night.

Our daughter Charmaine, was always welcome everywhere. Hers was the only presence that ever had any effect on Craig.

During the years when I was at home all day with Craig— Larry worked long hours and Charmaine was in school—Craig and I spent our days in exhausting battles. He would push me down the stairs and come after me with kitchen knives. When we finally locked all our sharp items in the trunk of our car, he broke a wooden desk chair by hitting me with it. It did not just break; it turned into splinters.

Then Charmaine would return home from school. Craig would still be wildly raging, and Charmaine would walk up to him and touch him gently on his arm, and he would instantly calm down. It was unbelievable.

Chapter 5:   Dancing to Happiness

Over the course of those early years, we learned from Charmaine's schoolteacher, her ballet teacher, and just about anyone with whom Charmaine came into contact that she brought calmness and peace to everyone around her.

I had always loved dancing. In junior high school, I took modern dance instead of physical education and found that I thrived while dancing, and I continued to dance all through high school. When I was in my late twenties and Charmaine was six years old, we signed up for ballet—she in beginning ballet and I in a class for ladies.

Going to the ballet studio was a real joy. For the very first time in many years, I had an outlet for my creative energy. It was wonderful to share the experience with our little daughter. After about a year and a half, I began teaching the beginning class for six- to eight-year-old girls. I also taught modern dance to the ladies.

At the age of seven, Charmaine was one of the little snowflakes surrounding the snow princess for the studio's Holiday Spectacular dance recital.

On December 26, 1974, we had a small party to celebrate Charmaine's birthday. All her special friends were there. As she opened her gifts and read her birthday cards, even our dog, Oliver, snuggled in close to be right in the middle of things. Now, as I look at snapshots from the party, with everyone smiling and having a great time, I can see that there was something different about our daughter—something hard to put into words or even to understand. She always seemed to be just a little bit separate from what was happening around her.

Chapter 6:   Moving to Our New Home

We had our first house built not far from where we had been living in a duplex, and we moved into our new home in early January 1975. Being a seamstress, I enjoyed making bedroom décor for both our children. Craig's room had a jungle theme, and Charmaine's featured a beautiful, soft floral print of lavender, pink, and white.

With our move to a house, Charmaine was able to return to the school where she'd gone to kindergarten. Her teacher at that time, Ms. Jones, had had a very special bond with our daughter. After teaching kindergarten for her entire career, Ms. Jones, upon learning of Charmaine's return to the school, changed classes to teach second grade so that the two of them could be reunited.

Our daughter was very happy in school that year. She was back at the school where she was most comfortable, and back with Ms. Jones.

We tried to attend church when we could, but that was difficult to do because the Sunday school class for very young children could not handle Craig, and so we did not attend often. Charmaine craved going to Sunday school, however, and one day Ms. Jones asked us if Charmaine could go to her church in order to attend Sunday school there. We agreed, knowing that this would make Charmaine very happy.

Chapter 7:   A Trip Back Home

In August 1974, we drove to Southern California to visit our families. We decided to take our two children to Catalina Island first, to visit my family. Neither of our children had yet been to the island, which held a very special meaning for Larry and me.

We lathered our red-haired, fair-skinned son with what seemed like gallons of sunscreen and set out for an afternoon at Avalon's tiny beach. Grandma and Grandpa came along, as did my sister. The beach was a great place for Craig to be free to run and play. Covered with long pants, a blue-and-white shirt, Grandpa's hat, and the essential sunscreen, he was quite a sight!

Charmaine looked as if she belonged there. She wore a little two-piece bathing suit I had made. It was a bright green and white print that showed off her golden tan and long blond hair. As she returned to our spot on the beach with a lime-flavored snow-cone, I saw a confident, happy seven-year-old girl. She almost glistened in the warm sunshine.

At the end of our beach visit, we all walked back up to my parents' house, having loaded up the little wagon with beach mats, colorful towels, and sand pails and other essential beach toys. Four-year-old Craig was determined to pull the wagon by himself back up to the house. This was quite a feat, as the long walk involved a slight but steady incline. Grandpa got a kick out of Craig's determination and strength.

Chapter 8:   Charmaine Is Ready

By the spring of 1975, we were settled into our new home. Easter of that year was quite cold and dreary. The outfits that I had made for the children were very cute but a little lightweight for them to be out hunting for Easter eggs. The warmth of spring had not yet arrived.

One weekend, Charmaine stayed overnight with her close friend, Marsha, whose family had moved out to the country. That Sunday morning, I drove out to pick her up and bring her back home. As we made our way back to town, Charmaine began talking about the purpose of Easter. She asked me when Jesus was going to return to Earth. I said that I was not sure. She then asked where he would be when he returned. Again I said that I did not know. Charmaine told me that she was afraid that she would miss Jesus. I told her that if she believed in him, he would find her.

As we continued the drive home, she became very quiet. She often became still in her own thoughts, with a very beautiful, peaceful look about her. At these times, she would have a soft, white light around her, and it almost seemed like she was somewhere else, somewhere I could not go. Now as I looked at her, I thought how very beautiful she was, inside and out. After about ten minutes, she turned to me and said, "But Mother, I am ready to be with Jesus now." Her statement did not frighten me, but I did notice that she had no fear or apprehension about this possibility.

Right at Easter, Craig came down with the chicken pox. Then the following week, as he recovered, Charmaine developed chicken pox. In those days it was normal to give children orange-flavored aspirin when they were sick, and so that's what I gave Charmaine. At the end of that week, Charmaine was recovering nicely, and since we had been cooped up in the house for two full weeks, we decided to go for a Sunday drive along the Lewis River in Washington, not far from our home. The sun was shining, but there was still quite a chill in the air. As we drove along, the song "Up the Lazy River" came on the radio. We thought that this was very appropriate.

The following afternoon, Charmaine told me she had a headache. When I asked her if she wanted an aspirin, she told me that the headache was not very bad. As the day went on, however, she began feeling worse. Her stomach became unsettled. That evening I stayed up with her while she vomited. When we tucked both children into bed that night, Oliver came into Charmaine's room with us, as he always did without fail. His routine was to jump onto her bed and stay as Larry read storybooks to her and Craig. This night, however, Oliver sat on the floor with his head resting on the edge of the bed. Even when we encouraged him to jump onto the bed, he chose to stay where he was. That was a puzzle.

By morning, Charmaine still could not keep even a tiny sip of water down. I called the doctor, who had me bring her to the office even before it was open. Thinking she had the flu, he gave her something to stop the stomach spasms. He said to give her tiny amounts of liquid, and that if she kept it down, to let her get some sleep.

All went as the doctor said, and so with Craig being in preschool, I decided to get some much-needed rest.

Suddenly Charmaine called out, "Mommy, I need you!" I went to her, but she did not respond to my presence. This continued off and on for a few hours. She then began thrashing about. I called the doctor, who told me that it was due to the sedative she'd been given.

I called Larry at work and told him what was going on at home. He was able to take off early to come and help me. When he arrived, we went in to check on our sick little girl. She looked pale and had very dark circles around her eyes. Larry called the doctor, and he had us meet him at the hospital.

Charmaine called out once again, and I returned to her and wrapped my arms around her as she tried to sit up. "Mommy, I am scared," she said.

I responded, "So am I, Charmaine."

She then settled back into quietness.

I held her on my lap as Larry backed the car down the long, steep driveway. Just as the car reached the road, I heard a voice tell me, "Now is the time to let her go." It was not a thought; this voice was very clear for me to hear.

As Charmaine lay in the hospital bed, I stood next to her, holding her hand. Numerous doctors, nurses, and lab techs did what they were meant to do: try to find out what was happening to this child.

It was April 15, but this year spring had not yet begun to show signs of arrival. Still, as I stood at Charmaine's bedside, something caught my eye—it was a beautiful white butterfly fluttering just outside the window. My attention quickly went back to my little girl, so helpless and now not responding to anything or anyone. I was probably there for one or one and a half hour, and the butterfly stayed the entire time, softly fluttering right at the window. I remember thinking how strange that was, as spring had not yet begun.

When Charmaine was moved out of the room for more tests, I joined Larry in an area where we had been instructed to sit and wait. This waiting room was in the maternity ward. Everyone around us was filled with joy and excitement. We were filled with fear and uncertainty. We were then ushered into a tiny room away from everyone.

Sometime around 11:30 p.m., we were told that Charmaine was being transferred to a hospital in Vancouver where a neurologist was on staff. We were told not to attempt to keep up with the ambulance on the forty-minute drive. Our friend Gene drove us to Vancouver.

At this new hospital, Larry and I were ushered into a small room to begin our wait. After what seemed an eternity, Larry left to find someone who could give us an update on Charmaine's condition. He was gone for so long that eventually I left that little isolated room and stepped out into the hallway. As I walked partway down the hall, not quite sure where I was headed, a doctor came toward me.

"Mrs. Powell, your daughter has Reye's syndrome," he said. "Her brain is swollen, her vital organs are failing, and we've put her on life support. She will not live." He then turned and walked away, leaving me alone. I leaned back against that cold, hard wall, trying not to collapse.

We stayed that night on hospital cots. Sleep was impossible. How could this be? Our precious Charmaine was gone. Just like that, matter-of-fact, over!

The next day, while Charmaine was on life support, the hospital chaplain came to us to pray. Apparently he could tell that I had no hope for her survival. When he asked me why, I said to him, "I know that Charmaine is already gone." He did not seem to understand why I would say such a thing. But deep in my soul, I knew that her soul had already transitioned.

Our dear friends Gene and Lucy stayed with us. Larry called our families, and they all headed for our home.

Our son, Craig, stayed at Gene and Lucy's house, where they and their teenage daughter cared for him.

On Thursday, April 17, 1975, life support was stopped for our baby girl. After two minutes and a few seconds, her beautiful body no longer functioned.

Chapter 9:   How Do We Go On?

When we returned to our home late that day, we were met by our family and friends. As I climbed the stairs to the living room, my mother was standing at the top and put out her arms to console me. I said, "No, don't," and I walked away.

There was nothing inside me to console.

Larry's dad offered to phone people to inform them of Charmaine's passing. He also offered to help Larry make the funeral arrangements. Larry turned down his father's offers, saying that he had to take care of everything himself.

I did not once go to the funeral home or the cemetery. I did attend the memorial service at our church; I knew that I could not handle the rest. To this day, forty years later, I still know that I would be incapable of that.

Our son, Craig, who was only four years old, was devastated. He was enraged that he had not said good-bye to his sister. He soon became very self-abusive—pulling his hair out, clawing at himself, and trying to jump out of a car and his second-story bedroom window. He was obsessed with death.

We took Craig to our pastor to have him talk to Craig about his feelings and thoughts. When the pastor said, "You seem to think about death a lot," Craig replied, "I have to. I have to prove what death is. I have to know what happened to my sister."

Our pastor told us that he had never known a four-year-old to analyze death to such an extent.

During that first year of learning to live without our angel, Charmaine, I experienced many, many times of total despair. One day while I was in the bathroom, standing at the mirror, I completely broke down, convinced that I could not go on another minute. I then noticed the beautiful fragrance of roses, and a soft, gentle breeze swirled around me. I felt completely enveloped; I felt caressed. I knew that I was not alone. It was a feeling of complete love, and I knew then that somehow I could continue through this life's traumas and ordeals.

Chapter 10: Visiting Love

Two years after our Charmaine died, I still longed to know if she was all right. Was her spirit missing me? Was she alone?

One night as I slept, in what seemed to be a dream, I found myself sitting in a wooden rocking chair in a pitch-dark space, desperate to have some answers. Suddenly a brilliant light appeared before me; it was so very beautiful. Then Charmaine was lying in my arms. Her eyes were closed and she did not speak to me with her voice, but there was mental communication between us. She told me that she was all right and that she was no longer in pain. Everything was wonderful. She was there to let me know these things, she said. I did not need to worry about her.

There was such a deep love between us that flowed throughout my body and soul. I did not feel that she was back; I knew that this was only a visit. But I knew that she was still our Charmaine.

The following day, Larry asked me what had happened to me in the night. When I asked him what he meant, he proceeded to tell me that during the night he he'd noticed that I was not breathing. He put his hand on my back, and not only was I not breathing, but I was also ice cold. My body is always warm, even my feet and hands. He called my name and I did not respond. Instead of panicking, he had the immediate thought that I had gone to be with our precious little girl. Then, slowly, my body returned to normal.

I then recalled that when I was in that special place, I heard Larry call my name and I told him, "I am all right. I am with Charmaine, and I am at peace."

Somehow we were not frightened by this experience. In fact, it was profoundly comforting. After that, I knew for certain that Charmaine was safe and that the love between us would never die.

Chapter 11: Outrage

For many years to come, when Craig would hurt himself, he would scream for me to help him, and then as I reached for him, he would attack me and yell, "Get your hands off of me! You kill children! You killed Charmaine!" I heard this accusation time and time again, sometimes several times a day.

Craig continued attending preschool at a local church. They handled him beautifully. Because he was so aggressive and disruptive, they would separate him from the other children and take him to a room with one or two teachers who would play with him. I felt such relief that I finally had someone to give me a break and also keep Craig safe.

One day we received a phone call from the school telling us that Craig had slammed into a support pole. We took him to the ER, where we were told that he had a concussion and needed to remain in the hospital overnight. After we knew that he was going to be all right, Larry and I thought we could have a reprieve for one night, a few hours of not having to worry about Craig. We went out to dinner, but I felt that I should be at home, enjoying the peacefulness of our quiet house.

Craig began kindergarten, going half a day, and fortunately his teacher was a six-foot-six man. Craig did okay at school that year.

At the age of eight, Craig was admitted to a Seattle hospital, where he was placed in the psychiatric ward for six weeks of testing and observation. We were advised to place him in residential care or a group home. I was both very sad and very relieved at this possibility. Maybe Craig could get the help he needed and I could get a part of myself back.

Larry could not do it. He felt that it would be as if our other child had died. I then knew that I had to endure much more of this nightmare.

Craig was placed in a special education class in public school. His teacher, Mr. Steve, was wonderful with Craig and truly took a special interest in him. Craig also liked Mr. Steve.

Since 1971, I had spent my nights being awakened by Craig's screams. The sounds that came out of him and his room were horrifying. Because there was no soothing him, I would sit in the living room with our precious dog, Oliver, by my side. That nighttime pattern became my normal for the next nine years.

Chapter 12: Craig Finds
a New Interest

One day Craig came home from school unusually happy. He announced that he had a girlfriend. His excitement was wonderful to see. Every day for about a week, his reports on his new love interest kept us all amused.

Then it happened: Craig came home upset, telling us his girlfriend dumped him. When we asked him why, he said, "She found out how old I am." The children in the special ed classroom were of different ages. His girlfriend was not in that classroom and had no idea that Craig was only seven. She was a couple of years older.

Craig announced, "Boy, I will never do that again."

"What?" I asked. "You will never go with an older girl?"

"No," he replied, "I will never let them know how old I am."

Craig's outbursts at school and at home were accelerating. His attack on another boy at school put the child in the hospital with a severe concussion. We were heartsick and frightened. After many agonizing days, we learned that the other child would be all right.

All our thoughts were focused on what would have happened if the boy had not recovered. What if he had died or had brain damage? Who would be next?

It was hard enough to interact with a child who attacked me. But when he was out in the world, attacking others, we could not intervene.

On one of the worst days I ever had with Craig, his rage and attacks went on nonstop for approximately five hours. As I was home alone with him, I used my human straightjacket technique on him for as long as I could physically hold on to him. He hit me with furniture, tried pushing me down the stairs, bit me, and tore up his clothing and bedding. He never wore down.

Late that afternoon, I just stopped. I stood in front of him and said, "Craig, you are trying to drive me insane, and I am not going to let you!"

He then stopped, stared into my eyes with a look of icy evil that went straight into my soul, and said, "But I am going to, and I know how." Calmly and quietly, he turned and walked away. I knew then that he could do what he said.

It was not until many years later that I could tell anyone what I experienced that day. Even today, as I write of this incident, I am chilled to my core.

Many times throughout the next several years, I felt that it would be so much better if I were no longer living.

One day when I was driving Craig home from his therapy session, as we were traveling on a two-lane road that paralleled a river, Craig began screaming over and over again, "You killed my sister. You killed Charmaine!" and "I hate you! I am going to kill you."

I reacted by saying out loud, "I cannot go through this one more time!" I was telling Craig, but mainly I was telling God.

There was not a barrier between the asphalt of the road and the embankment of the river. I turned the steering wheel of my car to the right. I had no fear, no anxiety. I felt at peace. Within a split second, the steering wheel gently turned to the left, and I was back on the road. The car stayed steady and smooth, and we headed home. Craig never said those words to me again.

Chapter 13: How Can We Go On?

As Craig's life of torment continued, I became more and more isolated and numb. I did not cry. I could not share the depth of our horrific lives with anyone. I felt no sadness, no joy, no anger, no fear or despair. I felt nothing! There was nothing left inside me. I was completely empty. That was the most frightening kind of existence. I knew Craig needed so much help, and I had nothing left within me to help him.

This poor little child broke my heart. He'd been given up by his biological parents, and his beloved sister had died. He seemed to be tortured by living, and even when he was acting relatively normal, I knew that at any second he could switch into a violent rage.

People were afraid of him. Specialists could not seem to help him. Medication was ineffective.

Was there anything or anybody that could help?

So I prayed—day after day, year after year—and continued to hope and wait for a miracle.

Chapter 14: The First Step to Finding Answers

Around the eighth year of Craig's life, his psychologist arranged for him to enter a hospital in Washington for six weeks of testing and evaluation. Larry and I would travel there each Friday to visit Craig and meet with the doctors who were working with him. We were interviewed, and of course the doctors needed to know what part we'd played in Craig's problems. It did not take long before they realized the gravity of his emotional state. They told us that Craig was extremely bright, and that he was capable of great manipulation.

He was put on high levels of Malarial and Thora zine. Nothing changed. The doctors said that in order for any medication to work, the required dosage would constitute an overdose.

Craig had always bitten his fingernails down to the quick. One of the times when he was confined to an isolation room, the staff checked on him and noticed blood on him. They went into the room and discovered that he had gouged at the peephole with his teeth and fingers because he was angry about being observed.

At times it took several of the well-trained hospital staff to physically restrain Craig. His rage and power were beyond comprehension.

At the end of this study, it was recommended that Craig be placed in a residential center for troubled children. But the expense involved was beyond our means, and insurance was no help because Craig suffered from a psychiatric disorder.

The state would cover half because Craig had been adopted from the state, but even paying half the cost was out of our reach.

What were we to do? The only other option was to bring him back home and continue this way of life. Our thoughts and fears about what might happen along the way, as Craig became older and stronger, were terrifying. And we would not be getting any additional help.

Nothing that I did seemed to help him. I had nothing left to give to him. All that we could possibly do to help him had been done. It was never enough.

It was amazing to see how this young boy could be so completely out of control and create such turmoil and then have a look of utter satisfaction on his face.

During one of Craig's stays at the hospital, the head of the psychiatric ward said that despite all their testing and observation, they were never sure whether Craig was truly out of control or knew exactly what he was doing to manipulate and control everyone around him.

Chapter 15: Some Happiness for Me

We continued on for the next two years. In the fall of 1980, Larry surprised me by telling me that he'd planned a trip for me to Catalina Island for a week's visit with my family. He was persistent, and I finally agreed to go. Larry would take a week off from work to take Craig camping.

Marsha and I talked about how we would take a couple of days and go to Santa Barbara—just the two of us! Then we decided that on the last day of that week we would go to an amusement park and fill ourselves with freedom and joy.

When I told my mother I was coming, I thought she would be glad to see me. But her response to the news was "Oh Gayle. How could you be so selfish? How could you do this to Larry?" I tried to tell her that this was Larry's idea and that he had planned everything, but she said, "I thought I raised you better than this. I am very disappointed in you."

Her reaction was not surprising to me, but I was hurt and disappointed. I put all that aside and focused on my plans for a week of relaxation and visiting my sister.

In Santa Barbara, Marsha and I shopped, ate at wonderful restaurants, and took in a couple of movies. The beautiful coastal town sparkled. The warm sun and the fresh sea air seemed almost magical.

As my sister and I were enjoying ourselves, I spoke on the phone with Larry. He had decided to drive with Craig to San Diego and visit my brother, his wife, and their teenage son, Rob. They would then travel up to the amusement park and meet us.

I almost panicked. I had just begun to relax, and now I was having to brace myself emotionally to be reunited with Larry and Craig.

When we got to the amusement park, I was afraid to turn a corner. Craig loved to scare me by jumping out at me and letting out an animal-like scream. I did not know where he and Larry were in the park; we were to meet them at a certain spot mid-afternoon. I think even Marsha felt the stress.

Finally, the time came to meet up with my family. I learned that while Larry and Craig were in San Diego, the money from Rob's paycheck had gone missing. They suspected Craig. Larry asked Craig about it, and of course he knew nothing about the missing money. Larry was quite concerned and felt bad for Rob. Rob was such a great young man; he was always so good to Craig, and Craig had always looked up to him. Larry searched Craig's belongings but found nothing that was not his.

While at the amusement park, Marsha offered to take Craig back on the boat with her to spend two days on the island, to give Larry and me some time together. It was such a generous offer. Larry and I headed back to Santa Barbara.

While Craig was in Catalina, my sister looked through his belongings. There it was: Rob's money rolled up in Craig's socks. I felt relieved that the missing money was found, but I was heartsick that Craig would do such a thing to his cousin.

Larry had put his heart and soul into believing in Craig. He'd always hoped and looked for the best in our son. Whenever Craig let him down, he would deal with the problem and then quickly move on, trusting that things would be better next time. But this time it was different.

Chapter 16: Larry's Breakdown

When Craig returned from the island and we began our long drive back to Washington State, Larry was unresponsive to everything concerning Craig: no talking, no anger, no physical or emotional connection at all. Any necessary communication—ordering food or taking bathroom breaks, but nothing else—had to go through me. Craig looked frightened by the lack of response from his dad. I knew that the severity of Craig's problems had finally impacted Larry to his core.

We drove for long hours, trying to shorten our time on the road. It was imperative to get Craig to a place where someone could help us all.

We stopped that night in Redding, California, and got a room at a hotel where we had stayed previously. Larry took care of all the necessary details, and I tended to Craig's basic needs.

Early the next morning, we packed up for another long, silent drive home and then stopped by the hotel restaurant for breakfast. Larry would not respond to Craig's food request, and so I placed my order and then told the server what Craig wanted. Before the food arrived, Craig took off running down the hallway. I tried to follow him, but I could not find him. Meanwhile Larry stayed put and continued eating his breakfast.

I panicked, not knowing whether Craig was in the hotel or outside, running away. Craig was not quite ten years old. I knew that we should call the police.

I returned to the restaurant, where Larry paid the bill for our mostly uneaten meal, and the two of us headed back to our room. Larry put the suitcases into the car and said, "Let's go!"

"We can't just leave Craig here," I said.

"Yes we can," he said.

But I refused to get into the car. "It's illegal to abandon him," I said.

Larry's behavior was unlike anything he stood for. He had shut down.

Craig finally showed up, and we headed north. I knew that somewhere in the back of my mind, I had wondered, *can we just walk away? Can we end this nightmare by just walking away?*

As we headed back, it was almost as if the air in our car were dead. Craig became withdrawn and slipped into one of his deep depressions. I was so frightened by what was happening to each of us. It was the same feeling of grief as when Charmaine died.

Chapter 17: Craig's Life Takes a Turn

There was no turning back now. Craig needed more help than what we were capable of giving him. Larry scheduled a meeting with Craig's psychiatrist, who arranged for Craig to be temporarily placed in the psychiatric ward of our local hospital. This was a ward for adult patients; our local hospitals had no facilities for children with severe emotional and behavioral problems.

I truly don't know if Craig was there for one night or three. All sense of time was gone. At some point Craig returned home, and we prepared for his journey north to be admitted to a residential center for troubled children.

Larry insisted on driving Craig there on his own. I was terrified that something disastrous would happen to one or both of them. Looking at this child who had terrorized me, I saw a very small, vulnerable little boy only wanting to be loved and protected. That is what I'd always wanted to do for him, but I could never find a way to reach him or be accepted by him. Now maybe someone else could fill his deep needs.

Larry and Craig arrived safely at the residential center. When Larry returned home, he seemed depressed and relieved at the same time. He said the facility was not exactly what we'd expected, but it was where Craig needed to be.

Our frequent two-and-a-half-hour travels there and back became a weekly routine. We never knew whether we could visit with Craig on these trips. Often he would have run off, or he would be out of control and not allowed out of a secure area.

On one visit in particular, Larry and I were scheduled to meet with Craig and a staff member and were asked to take a seat in the conference room. The room was dominated by an enormous, heavy table made of thick oak. There were also a few file cabinets and a coffee machine. Larry and I sat in some chairs at the far side of the room, with a wall of windows to our backs.

As some of the staff members brought Craig into the room, he exploded! He unleashed such fury that the full coffeepot flew across the room, shattering glass and spilling hot coffee everywhere.

Then Craig singlehandedly pushed that enormous table toward the wall of windows. As everyone turned to escape, Larry yelled at me to get out of there. I stayed in my chair, unemotional and quiet. I did not care what happened next. I had reached a state of existence as though even my soul had died. Craig pinned me against the wall with the table. Then he ran out of the room, continuing his rampage throughout the main offices.

Larry and the therapist pulled the table away from me. I was fine; I was not shaken. To me it was just another experience with this child.

The eighteen months that Craig was at this care facility were a blend of funny and terrifying events, of hope and despair.

Chapter 18: Craig Takes Over

We received a phone call at home informing us that Craig had barricaded himself in a bedroom with another boy. The previous night, while the other boys were sleeping, they had confiscated the TV and a stockpile of food from the common center. Now they were prepared for a long stay in their self-made bunker. Craig demanded to speak to the governor, stating that he would not come out until his demands were met. This was a twelve-year-old's version of Alcatraz!

The staff tried to get them out by various means, and then they thought better of it. Why should they try to get Craig out of there? They knew that he was safe and had food and a bathroom, and everything was so much more peaceful in the house without him among the other residents and staff.

This situation lasted about three days. Then the smell of smoke began to fill the air: Craig had set fire to the room. When firefighters arrived, they had to break into the room through the window, as there was no access through the bedroom door.

I don't know if Craig was upset that his demands were not being met, or if he got bored, or if he just wasn't getting the attention that he had hoped to get. Thank God no one was hurt and there was no major damage.

Our meetings with the counselors always left me feeling hopeless. We never received a positive report. Even though there was a school program for the young residents, Craig could not function in a classroom setting. He was extremely disruptive and violent. The staff decided that he would not attend classes anymore.

Finally, we were informed that Craig had to leave the facility. His therapist told us that while Craig was not the most dangerous child the staff had had there; he was by far the most complex child they had ever dealt with.

The therapist felt that a major part of Craig's rage stemmed not only from the death of his sister, Charmaine, but also from his being given up for adoption at birth. His feelings of abandonment consumed him. The therapist believed that Craig desperately needed some connection to his birth parents to begin his healing.

So the therapist began researching Craig's birth and adoption records. He was very surprised to find that the birth father's name was on the birth certificate, and that the man worked in our area. The therapist's plan was to work with Craig over a period of time in preparation for eventual contact between Craig and his birth father.

Around four months later, we received another call from Craig's therapist. He informed us that he'd come to realize that Craig was not ready to deal with this very emotional connection. He told us that Craig might not ever be able to face the issue. We were so deflated. We had hoped and prayed that this would be the key to helping Craig end his lifelong torment.

Chapter 19: Craig's Visit Home

Craig came home for the weekend from the residential care facility to celebrate his twelfth birthday. As any child would be, he was very excited about his birthday. And as everything was with Craig, his excitement was over the top. Because of his erratic and extreme emotions, there was never a middle ground.

As excited as Craig was for each birthday, he would completely fall apart with rage. He could not handle any celebration of his life. We learned to tone these events down to make them easier for him to handle. On this particular birthday, he wore dark-blue pants, a plaid shirt, and a rust-colored pullover sweater. He looked very nice.

We asked him to sit on the raised hearth of the fireplace so we could take his picture. We took two, a few seconds apart.

When the film was developed and we viewed the photos, the first one showed Craig with a very pained, angry look on his face. This picture is still very difficult to look at!

In the second picture, Craig has a beautiful, peaceful expression; it is perhaps the best photo ever taken of him. In this second photo, there is a soft, white light illuminating his right side. I assumed it was the light coming in from the large windows in the living room.

Later, during a therapy session I was attending, I showed the therapist those photos as an example of how very quickly Craig's emotions would change. The therapist was disturbed by the expression of hatred on Craig's face in the first photo. When she looked at the second photo, she paused for a moment and then said, "There is a spirit present in this photo." I explained that away by telling her about the large windows to his right. She replied, "So then, where is the white light in the first photo?" There was none.

After Craig had spent eighteen months at the first care facility, we were told that he could no longer remain there. They were losing staff members: Craig was burning them out; they could not deal with him. They would work on having him placed in another facility.

As discouraging as this news was, I felt something like relief—not because the arrangement had not worked out, but because it confirmed the seriousness of my struggles with Craig. I felt vindicated.

For twelve years, Larry and I had not only been criticized for how we were raising Craig, but we had also been told by some people that we treated Craig differently from the way we had Charmaine because she was our biological child. The fact is, if our biological child had had the same emotional and behavioral problems as our adopted child, our feelings and reactions would have been the same.

Craig was in desperate need of help. We were doing everything we could for him, and everything we could was never, ever enough. We were totally drained.

I was asked many times which was harder to go through, Charmaine's death or Craig's life. I could not answer that question easily, and the answer would not come for a long time. I knew that I would have relived our daughter's life and even her death over again, but I would never have chosen to relive Craig's life over again—not just because of the trauma that I was enduring, but also because it was heartbreaking to see a child in such torment.

We also lost so many relationships with family and friends. One very close friend, someone Larry had known since childhood and who was like a sister to him, wrote us letters, mainly to preach to us. In one letter she stated, "God took Charmaine from you as punishment for how you treated Craig!" At that point Larry reached his limit. He told me to just throw any future letters from her in the trash, unopened.

Whenever we tried to explain the situation that we were dealing with, the other people could not believe that a child was capable of such extreme behavior. Also, when he was with most people, he would put on quite an act. He was a master of manipulation; he knew exactly what he was doing.

I once asked him why he behaved totally differently with certain people. He replied, "I don't want them to know how I really am."

My stepfather really related to Craig; he almost seemed to cheer on Craig's rebellious nature. He truly loved both our children, but I think he could relate to Craig's frustration with life and with himself.

We were so isolated from others and also stripped of a normal life. We even had to protect our beloved family dog from Craig, and Craig loved Oliver.

Chapter 20: Craig Moves On

After Craig left the residential center, the state placed him in a foster home. His therapist and psychiatrist told the state not to place him anywhere near us or our community.

So the state placed Craig in a home in our very same town. I was terrified. It was arranged for Larry and me to meet this couple in their home. They seemed to be a caring couple, and their house was very nice. They assured us that they would take good care of our son. We were hoping for the best, but we were holding our breath.

The foster family had a teenage son and a cat in their household. The first report from them was that Craig was doing well and they were enjoying his company. They felt that their son, being older than Craig, could set a good example for him.

Well, it took a total of two weeks before Craig's social worker called and told us that he had been removed from the foster home. The family felt that Craig had stolen from their son and offered him marijuana. Craig was also belligerent and out of control. His behavior had become dangerous, and he committed a very serious offense that traumatized his foster family. Craig was removed from their home immediately.

Craig's psychiatrist knew that he needed a more secure placement, both for his own safety and for the safety of others. It was recommended that he be placed in a private extreme-care facility in the San Juan Islands. It was on a private island that was very isolated; the only access was by boat. The children could not leave the island. There was not even a town there.

We could not visit Craig on the island, but we would drive up and wait for the boat to arrive. Then we would take Craig out to lunch or to a nearby park. Sometimes we would make the long trek north to visit Craig and, for one reason or another, he would not be on the boat when it arrived from the island. I always had such apprehension on these trips. Each and every time, I felt hope, fear, and uncertainty about what we might be dealing with.

There were some visits that truly amazed me, when Craig was in an exceptionally good mood or acted very loving. But at any given moment, things could change without warning. I never had a clue what might happen or to what extent, and so I was always on guard. It was very difficult to live that way, and it also deprived Craig of the consistent love and nurturing that he longed for. I believe he needed to destroy any true connection before anyone else could destroy it. I don't think he ever felt safe or deserving of nice belongings or a secure home and family.

This would turn out to be the life we knew for many, many years to come.

Chapter 21: Craig Becomes an Adult

When Craig reached the age of eighteen, he was no longer considered a ward of the state. He was going to be released on his own, but fortunately his counselor arranged for him to be admitted into a work program in Oregon, not far from where Larry and I lived. We felt fairly safe, as Craig could not come and go at will. He was not to know our address or our phone number. All contact was to be initiated by us.

Our new home in Oregon felt like the gift of a new start in our lives. We were in a different house and even a different state, set apart from our previous home. From our new home we could view the sunset beyond the coastal range toward the west. Even on gray, cloudy days, right at sunset the clouds would usually break and the colors and light beams would put on a glorious show for us. Somehow I felt that this was a sign that our lives were going to improve and there was hope for us all.

Slowly I began looking forward to the future. I set up my sewing in a bedroom with a window that looked out onto the backyard. It was a very large yard with a beautiful, tall, old oak tree. The grass was lush, green, and well groomed. I usually sewed every day for the better part of the day. I thrived on working with fabric, enjoying the texture and of course the colors. I loved doing the fine detail work that I put into each garment or project for our home. I would play music I loved—Ella Fitzgerald was my favorite—and with our dog close by, I felt that I was set for a good day.

I have always been drawn to the aesthetic beauty of the Japanese culture, with its appreciation of serenity and balance. Our new home and its décor had many features of this culture, and we'd purchased a set of dishes that I felt blended in with this style. The set included one coffee mug that I felt I needed to use. On the outside it looked exactly like the others, but there was a very tiny crack just inside the rim. I think this mug represented more than I knew at the time.

I so wanted my life, our lives, to be beautiful and perfect, and even more than that, I wanted our lives to be normal. We could achieve "normal" on the outside, for others to see, but on the inside, our lives were flawed. As was the case with that little coffee mug, I assumed no one else would ever know about the defect.

It amazes me how we find ways to suppress our negative emotions in order not to appear different. I was taught from a very young age that I should always hide anything negative. I had many unfortunate experiences in my childhood, but I did as I was told: "Don't make waves!" "Don't get angry!" "Don't cry!" My mother instilled these rules in me, and I was a very obedient child.

Because Craig broke every rule and pushed every limit, I had an extremely hard time dealing with his behavior. Yet I admired his rebellious spirit.

Chapter 22: Stop!

One day while I was home alone, the phone rang. When I answered, there was no response at the other end and so I hung up. The phone rang again. Once again, no response from whoever had called. The pattern continued every day, Monday through Friday—never at night, never on the weekend.

After several weeks of this, I was becoming unnerved. I would leave the house and go to a neighbor's house. I was fearful of being home alone each afternoon. I told Larry what was happening, and I told him I thought Craig was making the calls.

"Why would you think that it is Craig?" he asked. "He doesn't have our phone number, or access to a phone."

I felt so alone and disillusioned. I had no one else to turn to with what I was experiencing.

Finally, one afternoon when the call came, I said to the silence on the phone, "Craig, I know this is you. Please talk to me or *stop* these calls!"

They stopped.

Chapter 23: Gayle's Life Takes a Hard Turn

For many years I had dealt with allergies, and as time went by I began to develop more and more symptoms related to my environment. By the late 1980s, I was having persistent respiratory infections. After being treated with repeated rounds of antibiotics, I was referred to an immunologist, who put me through all the usual testing to pinpoint the various offenders. Then the treatments began.

I spent the next several years taking allergy shots but never could build up an immunity to my allergies. The infections continued and consistently got worse. The doctor had me on powerful doses of antibiotics and prednisone. This pattern continued for almost eight years, and still I got weaker and sicker. There were times that I had to crawl up the stairs in our home. I had no appetite, but I kept on gaining wright.

My sleep pattern was completely messed up. I was exhausted yet could sleep only two to four hours a night. This nighttime pattern reminded me of my life when Craig was at home. I felt a deep sense of despair and desperately needed a way to solve the problem. It was scary not knowing what was causing my decline, and there did not seem to be any hope for a resolution.

Because Larry's insurance covered naturopathic care by a certified doctor, I decided to give this treatment a try. I found a doctor of natural medicine in the neighboring community. After a very thorough exam and much questioning, the doctor said he believed that he could help me.

He felt that years of severe stress had taken their toll on me and that my immune system was shutting down. He told me that I had "the metabolism of a slug."

I responded, "Do you mean it is *that* good?"

Around this time, I developed a strange patch of skin on the middle of my back. It was completely white, and it itched nonstop. After seeing several specialists, all of whom were as puzzled as I was, I went to see yet another dermatologist.

As soon as she saw this strange patch of skin, she exclaimed, "Oh, this is morphea!" She explained that this very rare condition was caused by someone's immune system turning against him or her. It could appear anywhere on the body, and if it developed internally, it was usually fatal.

Why this news brought me relief, I am not sure. I suppose that finally having a medical reason for what I was experiencing—proof that I wasn't imagining it—made me feel validated.

Our bodies let us know when they have reached their limits. I suppose that if I were the type of person that could easily exhibit her emotions, I probably would have been able to release some of the stress that had built up inside me.

I tend to hold everything in, and I don't want others to judge me by my emotions. A lesson I learned at a very early age was that everything should appear fine on the surface even if things were falling apart on the inside. I was still trying so hard just to hold on—hold on to my family, hold on to my health, and just hold on to who I was. I don't think that I even knew who this person called "me" was anymore.

Chapter 24: Craig Is on His Own

After Craig was released from the work camp, he was on his own. At one point he was admitted to a center of some kind, maybe a halfway house, not far from our home in Oregon. We received a call that he had gone on an emotional rampage and had to be physically restrained. Apparently it took six well-trained men to do it. Craig's strength when he became violent was overwhelming to anyone.

Nevertheless, my fear of what Craig might do to me had diminished over the years. The threat was still there, but it seemed less important to me now.

For the next several years, we had sporadic visits with Craig. One time when my parents were visiting us in Oregon, he decided to drive down from up north to see them. He had purchased a small truck, and he seemed excited to visit his grandparents.

It was a very good visit. Craig's Grandpa Frank was especially happy to see him doing well. There was no drama—no rages or damage. This was a very welcome visit for all.

Not long after that, we found out that Craig no longer had his vehicle. To me it was pointless to ask him what happened. We heard from Craig regularly about the many and various jobs he was working, along with where and how he was living.

One Christmas, Larry wanted Craig to come for a visit, and so he arranged for Craig to take the bus down to Portland. Our time together was very tense. Craig was not eating much, and he was restless and shaking. He was so out of sorts that it really scared us, so Larry took him to the ER at our local hospital. After one look at Craig, the doctors told Larry that Craig was a drug addict and there was nothing they could do for him.

Larry then took Craig to the airport, bought a one-way ticket north, gave him fifty dollars, and said good-bye. While Larry's good heart hoped that he was helping his son, we both knew that the money would go toward his next fix.

It is so exhausting to want your loved one to be able to live a healthy, happy life but to realize that everything you do for him is in vain. One of the hardest lessons I had to learn in life was that I could not always protect the ones that I loved from death or suffering. But I always tried. I could only hope and pray to God for help and protection. It would still be a long time before we saw a glimmer of hope. I truly had shut down my emotional involvement with Craig.

Chapter 25: Surprise!

In 2000, Craig called us to announce that he was engaged. Our question was "Do you even *know* a girl?" He told us that he had become involved in a church not far from his birthplace and gotten close to the assistant minister and his family. This young woman was the minister's daughter.

They were married in February, after a very short relationship. Soon they were expecting a baby. Our hope was that Craig would finally have a family with which he could feel that he belonged.

Upon receiving the news that Craig's wife was in labor, Larry and I got in the car and headed up north. Our grandson entered this world before we got to the hospital. There was a medical emergency, and for a while his health was uncertain, but by the next day all was good. Our hearts were touched by Craig's gentle love toward his new baby son.

This new member of our family was a very sweet, good-natured baby. He had the most beautiful eyes. I felt closer to Craig by loving his son. I could play with this little baby, and even nurture him. It almost seemed that I was able to give my love and care to our son through his child.

As we'd anticipated, Craig's marriage was riddled with difficulties. Both parents loved their son deeply, but that love was not enough to overcome the disorders that controlled their lives.

Craig's wife and in-laws were heavily involved in their church, which was very fundamentalist. Larry and I felt that this served as a positive influence on Craig, providing him the healthy foundation he seemed to need.

What then followed was Craig preaching to Larry and me about the way we lived our lives. He felt that if we did not follow the teachings of his faith, we were not Christians. Larry and I have always felt that how you live your life and how you treat others, including animals and nature, is more important than dogma.

Chapter 26: A New Start

Not long after Craig's marriage ended, we received a call from him. He announced that he and his new girlfriend—a woman we had met only once—had just gotten married. As usual, Craig was over the top with excitement. This marriage would last only a short time.

And so Craig was once again single. He seemed to stay involved in his son's life as much as was allowed. He always spoke of his son with pride and love, but the power of drugs in his life always won.

His erratic pattern of functionality continued: he would be working and then not working; there would be regular visits from him and then no word from him for long periods of time.

As had been the case most of his life, we never knew where Craig was, how he was, or even if he was still alive. Sometimes knowing was more emotionally difficult than wondering about him. For me it was extremely painful to love someone and worry about him, yet fear him.

Chapter 27: Twelve Steps to Success

Craig connected with a twelve-step program when he was about forty years old. Apparently he had tried other programs first but felt more comfortable with this one. That was mainly due to his sponsor, Don. Although Craig told us that he was attending this group's meetings, we learned little else about it for a couple of years.

Our connections with Craig became more frequent. He seemed to be developing a more caring attitude toward us, and especially toward me. Craig and Larry could almost always relate to one another, so the change in their relationship didn't seem quite as dramatic.

To my utter surprise, Craig acknowledged me on Mother's Day, and then again on my birthday. His actions seemed sincere and loving. He and I started having phone conversations about various matters, and I began to notice a real connection between us. His moods started to mellow. He did not seem to be full of rage. I began to relax, and I truly enjoyed the new relationship developing between us.

Craig would share with us a little news at a time about his life and his involvement with the twelve-step program. Then he told us that he had met a lady he liked. She was single and had no children. Their friendship continued to develop, and he seemed happy. One thing that was different with this relationship was that it was progressing at a more normal pace. We did not detect any of the chaotic rush to get married, fortunately for Craig's son. This made us more comfortable.

Craig's new girlfriend was well educated and had many interests. The two of them seemed to balance each other out.

One of the best things about Craig is his personality. He is enthusiastic, exuberant, and very funny. We are now seeing these qualities begin to blossom. His extreme mood swings are fading away. He is finding peace within himself and acceptance of and love for others. It is so very wonderful to get to know the person who has been beneath all that turmoil since infancy.

After Craig lost his first company he once again owns his own business. When Larry had the opportunity to be with Craig as he was working with a prospective client, Larry was extremely impressed by the way Craig interacted with this person. He was straightforward and honest. He knew his craft well and came across very professionally. The prospective client was sold on what Craig proposed. Craig seems to know instinctively how to deal with others and has a great business presence. Larry was proud of him, as I was upon hearing of this experience.

Craig has steadily continued along this upward path. He gained custody of his son and has grown into an amazing father who is very involved in his child's life. He disciplines with honesty and always with love.

With this wonderful lady in his life, Craig has been learning about healthy eating—just one more way that he is now taking an interest in his own well-being. Every step toward taking better care of himself is so positive and helps confirm his steady transformation to living a better, more productive life.

Because I was a florist for eleven years, Craig knows how much I enjoy flowers. For several years now, he has had very large, beautiful tropical floral arrangements delivered to me. So much thought and love goes into these gestures. I truly feel the emotions Craig expresses through his interactions with me.

Chapter 28: A Very Special Fiftieth Wedding Anniversary

Over the years, we have had many beautiful experiences that have let us know that we are surrounded by love. One such experience came on our fiftieth wedding anniversary.

We were in Palm Desert for the week, enjoying the warmth that is not available in January where we live in the Northwest. It was a beautiful day, and the sunshine seemed to warm not only our bodies, but also our souls. On this trip, I asked Charmaine's spirit to let us know that she was with us.

Larry and I drove to La Quinta, California, to have lunch and to visit the area, with which we were not familiar. After lunch we drove around this small community, which offered shops, restaurants, and beautiful landscaping. As we drove down one street, we noticed a hedge with beautiful orange flowers in bloom. Larry circled the block and found a small parking lot right across from the hedge so we could walk across the street for a close-up picture.

I stayed in the car with the windows down and the radio playing. As I sat there in the sunshine, the song "Charmaine" came on the radio. I was anxious to tell Larry about what had just happened. When he returned to the car, he found a penny right on top of the console between our seats. He said, "Here is a penny from heaven."

As we sat there absorbing these two meaningful experiences, a white butterfly fluttered in my window and lingered for quite a while directly in front of my face. Then, with gentle grace, the butterfly slowly returned to the beauty outside.

"I don't even know whose parking lot we are in," Larry said. He looked for a name on the closest building: the business was named Angel.

I thanked our Charmaine for all the signs she'd given us on our anniversary. Not only were we warmed by the sunshine, but our souls were warmed by this precious experience.

We have been blessed by moments like these time and time again. We have learned to pay attention to these gifts and to be very thankful for them. Our faith deepens with each and every one of these moments, and we no longer pass them off as mere coincidences.

Chapter 29: My Wildest Dreams

For forty years I could never in my wildest dreams have imagined that Craig and I would reach this stage in our relationship. I am now able to experience a complete family.

Larry and I are still together, despite traveling through the deepest grief after our Charmaine Noel died, and despite many years of enduring Craig's horrific struggles in life. The one constant in all of this has been our trust that God would get us through it.

There are many levels of faith or belief systems. We have never been the type of people to preach to others or brag about our faith or beliefs. For me there is a deep connection between my belief in God and what my life experiences have been.

When we've shared our life experiences with others, we have seen how people listen with their hearts. Our story seems to affect them on a very deep level, as though our souls are touching. Each and every connection on this level has stayed with me, and I am very blessed to have had these experiences. I am grateful for these gifts of life.

I have such great hope for our family's future together. And so, our journey continues.

Part Two

By Larry Powell

Chapter 1:   One Step at a Time

My first recollection of Gayle was in church in the early 1960s. I was sitting with a friend who asked me if I knew the girl a few rows ahead of us. I said that I did not but would like to—although, as I later found out, she was a grade above me in school. I knew there was little chance of a sixteen-year-old like me having any kind of relationship with an older girl. I was tall and skinny, with dark-rimmed glasses and what I thought was a cool flattop. I was not the smartest kid, but I could make people laugh. Laughing is one of my best attributes. I had not yet had what you could call a full-out date with any girl, younger or (certainly not) older.

Gayle was the girl that my two-year-older brother knew. He had said that she was nice to be around and had dated some of his friends. To me, she was the girl that I had very little chance of getting to know well, let alone date.

Gayle and her friends were organizing a beach party to be held in just a week. She and her friends were trying to get me a date for the party, but I was not interested in the girl they suggested. Gayle had a date, but he canceled a few days beforehand because he had to go out of town with his father. So everybody thought it would be a good idea for Gayle and me to go together.

It was not what you would call a romantic first date. I spent most of my time in a watermelon fight with some strangers on the beach, and I spent the rest of the time trying out my martial arts skills on several girls at the party—or as Gayle tells the story, I was tripping them. Why? Because I was sixteen, and it seemed like the thing to do to impress her.

For a while, Gayle and I stayed somewhat connected, seeing each other at church functions and in school. I was the boy who rode his bike several miles to Gayle's house to visit her. Her mother could not understand why Gayle was interested in this boy when he did not even have a driver's license, let alone a car.

Six months later, I worked up the courage to try to kiss her. It was more of a missed kiss than what you would consider a romantic first kiss. So went the rest of our five years as a couple. Gayle went on to junior college near her home and joined the dance team. She had taken modern dance in high school and loved it. We went to some school dances together, but I never reached the level of her skill and grace. She loved the grace involved in dancing, while I liked the active dances popular at that time. Years later she would take, and eventually teach, ballet.

When we married on January 30, 1965, the wedding was more like a business event for my parents. There were 450 guests in all: some family and friends and a lot of my parents' business associates. It was not the romantic event we had hoped for, although the wedding itself was almost as beautiful as Gayle was that day. We honeymooned in the mountains above Palm Springs, California, where we had expected to enjoy a snowy weeklong romance. As with so many things in our lives, it was not as we had hoped. The donkeys corralled behind our cabin made noise all day and all night long. We cut short our week to three days and happily went home to set up our first apartment.

We both wanted children early on. In the sixties, most newlyweds had a baby within the first year or so of marriage. We had moved to a six-unit duplex that had five other new families with young children and more on the way. That life was not to be for us. I had a low sperm count, and we tried every conventional and unconventional method to get Gayle pregnant. Finally, the doctor gave me some hormone shots that did not work until well after the injections.

Then our first miracle came upon us: the shots finally worked. We were very happy to learn that Gayle was pregnant.

At the time, my parents were in Hawaii for their twenty-fifth wedding anniversary celebration. We were supposed to pick them up at the airport, and Gayle said that we should wait to tell them the news until we got them home. But the second we saw them working their way through the crowd after disembarking, I yelled at the top of my voice, "We are pregnant!" Everybody in the crowd turned to see who was shouting out with such happiness.

Gayle's pregnancy went very well. She was healthy but did not show very much. While we did not know whether it was a girl or a boy, Gayle felt it was going to be a very special girl. I enjoyed laying my head and hands on Gayle's stomach to feel our baby kick and move. This baby was truly going to be a blessing from God.

Gayle was due at the beginning of 1967. During the 1966 Christmas holidays, our family members were making bets on when Gayle would deliver.

In the sixties, few hospitals would allow fathers in the delivery room. But we felt that the birth of our child was going to be a very special time in our lives, and we really wanted me to be part of it. I finally convinced the hospital administrator to let him see how I would react in the delivery room.

It was the joy of my life to see Charmaine Noel born on December 26, 1966. I felt that my time alongside Gayle during the delivery reflected the true meaning of love between two people who had tried so hard to get to this point. Charmaine was beautiful and healthy. She and Gayle were doing so well that we were able to take Charmaine home the next day. As we were getting ready to leave the maternity ward, I nervously stepped back against a decoration that had Christmas ornaments on it with a new baby's name on each one. They came crashing down, but known of them broke. The nurses had dressed Charmaine up in a large Santa hat. It was time to take our Christmas baby home.

Chapter 2:   Family

Fortunately, we both agreed that Gayle should be a stay-at-home mom. We worked hard to live on the income I made in the printing business. Each day of Charmaine's infancy, I could see the love and bonding between mother and daughter. I could never understand how other mothers could leave their children during the day just to have more unimportant "things." This was the time of our lives that brought us closer together than we'd ever thought possible.

Charmaine was an angel in every way (our definition of an angel: a messenger from God). She brought joy to everyone she came in contact with. Little did we know that this was to be the case for the rest of our lives.

Six months after Charmaine was born, I was misdiagnosed with the mumps and ended up in the hospital with a 104-degree fever. Sometime after my release, we discovered that there was absolutely no chance of another pregnancy. We wanted more children, and so we started the adoption process. We knew it was going to take a long time, but we were happy to wait for our next child. We had asked that the baby be a boy, and that he not have red hair or a fair complexion. Being a Southern California family, we spent a lot of time at the beach, and we did not want to deal with the issues of a low-sun-tolerance child.

We were not aware of the time this would take. During that time, we considered moving to the Northwest, where we could afford a house on the income that I was making as a printing pressman. It would also be an opportunity to separate from our families and start our own lives as we saw fit. We had not heard anything for a long time from the adoption agency, and so we started the process of finding work in an area that we thought would be a wonderful place to raise our family. We went to the library to research all the cities in the Northwest that looked like a good possibility. I sent out several résumés and had several offers. We took a week's vacation to go to the companies in which I had a lot of interest. I interviewed with the most promising companies in larger cities and a few small towns. We decided to take an offer in a town called Longview, Washington, population thirty thousand. What a difference from Los Angeles!

I was offered a job not as a pressman, but as a sale representative, although the position was not going to be available until the following year. We returned to Southern California, where I continued on with the same company where I'd already worked for six years.

The Longview company called me one year later with an offer. This seemed to be a good direction for our family. I moved first, living in Longview for a month before bringing Gayle and Charmaine to our new home. During that time, the adoption agency called Gayle to say that they had found a baby for us. However, we would not be able to move to Washington during the yearlong adoption process. We decided to move anyway and start the process over in the state of Washington.

We moved into a duplex just a few miles out of town. I passed one stoplight and one stop sign getting to work. What a difference from the freeways of LA! It was not unusual for me to come home to have lunch with Gayle and Charmaine.

We started the adoption procedure in May of that year. In November, we received a call from the state adoption agency saying that they had found a boy for us; he was just a few weeks old. But they said there was a problem: the baby had red hair and light skin, which was not our desire according our original paperwork from California. We explained that we had made that request when we were in LA, and now that we were living in the Northwest, the sun was not a factor. We were just excited to have this opportunity so soon.

We took a four-hour drive north to see the newest addition to our growing family. We were asked to check into a particular motel, and agency staff would bring the baby to us the next morning. When they arrived, all three of us were so excited to meet our new son/brother. The agency left the baby with us for the day and came to pick him up in the evening. They said that they would bring him back the next morning. If we were not there, they would know we did not want him. We were there with open arms.

Charmaine held the baby while sitting on the edge of the bed. When the agency representative asked if we wanted to keep him, Charmaine spoke out first in a strong voice: "He is ours!" And so he was—all ours, and such a loving and cuddly baby. We were so happy that he was healthy and really liked to eat. We were over the moon with joy over our son, whom we called Craig.

Chapter 3:   Sometimes Love Comes in a Strange Package

Craig was our dream come true. He was healthy and bright, and he ate like a horse. Charmaine enjoyed being the big sister in every way. She helped Gayle with Craig and with a lot of the chores around the house.

In September, we got a puppy that we named Oliver. Soon Christmas was upon us, and we all went out in the snow to cut our own Christmas tree. That was a first for us, being from LA.

Three months after Craig joined our family, Gayle and I were in the living room for the evening when we heard a scream coming from Craig's room. We went in to check and saw that his lips were blue and he was not breathing. We picked him up and gave him a little shake. He would take a few slight breaths after a few continuous shakes. We rushed him to the hospital, and doctors were able to get him to breathe on a regular basis. After numerous tests, they still did not know the cause of the episode, but later they admitted that if Craig had died, they would have listed the cause of his death as SIDS.

We were so happy when Craig was back in the arms of his family, although we started noticing a difference in him. Suddenly he did not like to be held, and he would fight us off when we tried to feed him. Each meal was a struggle to get him to eat. When he eventually did, he would eat three to four times the amount that

Charmaine had when she was that age. Craig was a large baby—not fat, just solid.

On top of his refusal to be held or fed, he also had difficulty sleeping. From the time he came home from the hospital until he was four or five years old, he slept an average of two hours a day, and he rarely took a nap. By the time he was one, he would fight to get out of his crib, even to the point of jumping up and down to knock the frame and mattress out of the bottom of the crib. He would then get out of his room, even at night. We finally had to put a latch on the outside of his door. One time when Gayle went to check on him, he had moved his crib up against the wall, opened the window, and climbed halfway out. We finally nailed his crib to the floor in the middle of the room and bolted the window so it opened just a few inches.

Our doctors kept close tabs on Craig and tried to help us with him as much as possible. Because he was not getting much sleep during those years, neither was Gayle. One doctor, after trying whatever children's medications where available, told us to give him a drop of brandy. When that did not help, he suggested that Gayle take it. Nothing worked for either Craig or Gayle. Somehow both Charmaine and I were able to sleep through most of the noise that Craig was making.

Both Craig and Charmaine loved our dog, Oliver, who was large enough to handle Craig's roughness. He was also very comforting to Gayle and myself. He was a mix of Norwegian elkhound and standard poodle. (Charmaine would tell people that he was three-quarters Norwegian elkhound and one-quarter lovable.) Oliver was everybody's dog. He would play rough with Craig and gently with Charmaine, and be lovable and protective with Gayle. I just enjoyed him, even after he chewed down the first tree I ever planted. When I came home from work, all that was left was a six-inch stub of that five-foot tree.

When Craig was old enough, we entered him into a day care program, partly for educational reasons and partly to give him personal interaction with other children his age. It would also give Gayle a breather. We tried him at several different day care facilities, always with the same result: within a short period of time (hours), Gayle would get a call to come and get him and not bring him back. He was so difficult to handle that the staff at these facilities were not willing to work with him. We finally found a church day care that would dedicate one or two staff members strictly to Craig.

During this time, we did have wonderful moments when he was calm, loving, and well behaved. That always gave us hope that these times would increase. We would go as a family to the mountains and play in the snow, and in the fall we would go to the park and pile up leaves to jump in. Craig, Charmaine, and Oliver would bury themselves in the leaf pile, and I would pretend not to be able to find them. These times would also give Gayle a breather.

Chapter 4: Charmaine the Big Sister

During these first four years with Craig, Charmaine was a big help in so many ways. She had the ability to calm him down with just a touch of her hand on his arm or back. She enjoyed playing with him in the yard, and that always included Oliver plus neighborhood friends. Our swing set was a big hit in the neighborhood.

Charmaine was a good student and enjoyed going to church. She preferred going to another church with one of her teachers, as it was difficult for her and us when Craig raised a commotion during church services. She also enjoyed taking ballet lessons. In one of her ballet recitals she was dressed like a snow fairy but looked like and danced like an angel. Gayle also took ballet lessons and eventually taught ballet to young children. Dance was a good outlet for both of them, and they enjoyed every moment of it.

As soft and gentle as Charmaine was, she also had an active side that came out when she rode the horse on springs that we got her. When she rode it, it would shake the house. She particularly enjoyed riding it when she was dressed up in her cowgirl outfit, including her cowgirl hat. That horse lasted for years, and riding it was one of her favorite things to do. When Craig got large enough, he also enjoyed this activity.

In 1974, we bought a three-acre piece of land at the end of a road not far from where we were living. It was a hillside property that had a year-round running creek between the road and where we planned to build our new house. It was also backed up by forestland, so we knew there would never be anybody living behind or on the west side of us.

The hillside and creek were favorite play areas for our children. We had the house built as a split-level and did not finish the lower level with the exception of the bathroom. The rest of this lower area became a play area for our children and their friends during the winter. The forest behind us was a blessing, especially for Craig. He would spend hours in that forest and always came home tired.

There were happy times with Craig as well. He did have his good side on occasion, and he was very funny at times. But even when things were going well with Craig, it was hard for Gayle and me to enjoy ourselves knowing that at any minute he would change back into the difficult child he could be. I was the one who would fall the hardest for his good side. Then when he changed, it really hurt me. When Craig was good, I would hope and pray that he would just stay that way. It was not to be.

He enjoyed his Big Wheel. Our driveway at the new house was very long and steep and made of gravel—the perfect setup for Craig to go as fast as he could downhill. When he got to the bottom, where the driveway met the street, he would spin out. We lived in the last house on our side of the street, which was a dead end, and so he was able to see if there was traffic coming from a long way away. He also played with Hot Wheels a lot. Lincoln Logs were his favorite indoor pastime. He could not get enough logs to build what he wanted. Over time we bought more and more logs for him, and he would build the most unusual structures on our raised fireplace hearth. Many times the structures would extend over the edge of the hearth. We still don't know how he did this without them collapsing.

When Craig was about four or five years old, we would buy a two-foot-long piece of four-by-four and several pounds of three-inch nails, and he would spend hours in the garage pounding nails into the wood with my hammer. Those were some good times.

Gayle had designed Charmaine's room just the way she wanted it. She was so happy, and she had many friends over to play in her room. I made Craig's room the way he wanted it. He wanted his bed built up high so he could have a play area under the bed as well as on top. His room became his playground.

Gayle decorated the house just the way we liked it. We even had a view of Mount St. Helens. My dad designed and helped me build a deck on the back. It was a very private space with the forest just behind us. It was a dream home come true.

Chapter 5:   Charmaine Noel Powell

A few months after we moved into our new home, Craig came down with the chicken pox. Several children in the school and our neighborhood had it. A few weeks after Craig began doing better, Charmaine got chicken pox too.

On Easter she felt good enough to go to church with her teacher. We found out later that she went forward to receive Jesus Christ as her savior on that Easter Day. Several days later, however, she had a hard time keeping down food and water. Gayle kept her home from school that morning and took her to the doctor, who gave her a mild sedative to calm her stomach. She was doing better and lay down to take a nap.

I came home early that day, around four o'clock. Craig was in day care that day. Gayle said that Charmaine was taking a nap and seemed to be doing better, and so I went to her room to see how she was doing. She seemed to be in a deeper sleep than normal. I tried to wake her, but she would not wake up. I wondered if she was in a coma. I called the doctor, and he said to take her to the hospital and he would meet us there. So we picked her up and rushed her to the hospital. Thank God that Craig was in day care on that particular day.

The doctors at the hospital did test after test on Charmaine. At one point there were seven different doctors working over her. I was in the room with her and all those doctors for what seemed an eternity. They told us that her kidneys and liver were failing.

After about four hours of tests and trying to help her, they contacted a neurologist at another hospital about an hour away; he wanted her to be transferred to him. They put her in an ambulance, and our family doctor rode with her to the other hospital.

Our minister and some friends had been with us for most of our time in the first hospital. Now our friend Gene drove us to the new hospital while his wife, Lucy, went to pick up Craig and take him to their house. We arrived about fifteen minutes after Charmaine and her doctor. When we walked in, the neurologist met us in the hallway. He told us that Charmaine had Reye's syndrome. We had never heard of it. He said that it was fatal. She was brain dead, but they had her on life support just as a precaution.

We were distraught. We could not believe what had happened to our daughter in such a short period of time. When we were told this terrible news, I fell against the hall wall and slid down, crying. I really don't remember much after that.

Meanwhile Craig was staying with our friends' teenage daughter near our home. He had no idea what was going on, and neither did anyone else.

We stayed the night at the hospital, trying to sleep in a waiting room. I don't know if either of us got any sleep. It didn't really matter. We had lost our daughter, and that was the only thing we could think about. In the morning, the doctor came to us and recommended that they keep her on life support for twenty-four hours and test for brain activity again, just to make sure. They said it was our choice whether and when to turn off the life support. I could not think of turning off our daughter's life support. That was not something we or anyone could have been prepared for. Was it like turning off a light switch, and then it was all over? *Please, God help us*, I kept praying over and over.

I called our family doctor, who was back in his office that morning. I asked him to help us make a decision about what to do. We were both in shock from this horrifying situation. He said that legally, as a doctor, he could not help us with that decision. Our doctor was as good a friend as anyone to our family, and especially to Charmaine. I could tell this was eating him up as much as it was us.

Charmaine stopped having brain activity on April 15, but because she was on life support, they pronounced her legally dead on April 17. To this day, on both of those dates we remember Charmaine and the life she shared with her family and friends.

When I called my parents in California and told them what was happening, it was hard getting the words out. They left immediately to fly up to be with us. I also called a friend who knew Gayle's mother and stepfather. We were worried that if we called them with this news, they would not handle it very well. Our friend flew over to Catalina Island, where they lived, and helped them get to Los Angeles to catch a flight to Portland, near where we were.

We made the decision to turn off life support on Charmaine before they arrived. It seems strange to say that we were fortunate in some ways. In our state, the parents of a brain-dead child can make that decision. In some states at that time, it was up to the courts to make that decision. Within just minutes of the time they turned off the life support system, Charmaine's fragile body gave in.

We knew that Charmaine was in heaven, just as she'd believed she would be. She was with Jesus, just as she'd said she wanted to be. While we were in Charmaine's hospital room, Gayle looked out the window and saw a white butterfly fluttering around the window for an extended time. During that time of year, you do not see butterflies. We believe that it was Charmaine's spirit letting us know that she was in a good place and wanting us to always remember her. Even after all these years, when we see white butterflies, we always remember Charmaine.

Chapter 6: Home without Charmaine

I am not sure how we got back to our home, which by then was full of family and friends. Craig was there too by the time we arrived. I took him into his bedroom and told him that Charmaine was in heaven with Jesus. He was four years old and not sure what all this meant, except that he would never see his sister again.

I needed to make funeral arrangements, and my father offered to come with me, but I told him no thanks—this was something I needed to do on my own for our child. As Charmaine's father, it was up to me to make the decisions with Gayle about how we would get through the next few days. I did not realize how hurt my father was by my response. Months later, my mother told me that he broke down on the flight home. He told her that my refusal to let him help reflected what he had taught my brother and me: to be independent and make our own choices. He said that he wished he had not taught his sons to be so independent. I have always felt bad about my decision to handle this myself, but it seemed like the right thing to do at the time.

I went to a funeral home where I knew the owner through business relationships. He was a tremendous help. I know he had children of his own, and he really helped me though the process at a time when I was not thinking very well. He said he would go himself to get Charmaine and bring her back to us.

Gayle and I had talked about our wishes for Charmaine's funeral. We would have a viewing that could be attend only by our family members. We also wanted to have the funeral just for our family and a few close friends.

Gayle picked out one of Charmaine's favorite dresses, one that Gayle had made for her for square dancing. I took it to the funeral home with me.

The next day, our family went to the viewing. Gayle did not want to see Charmaine; she wanted to remember her as a healthy, beautiful little girl. I took Craig separately so he could see that Charmaine was at peace. We both touched her to say our good-byes. She looked as beautiful as she had when she was dancing ballet as a snow angel. We both cried and took our time with her.

Our minister knew Charmaine very well. I am sure it was very hard for him to give the sermon at the funeral. I honestly don't remember much of that day.

Charmaine was laid to rest at a local cemetery. With us were just the family members who had traveled there for the funeral and a few close friends who had attended the memorial service in our church. Gayle was present for the funeral but did not go to the cemetery. I wished that I did not have to go either, but it was my duty to go as her father, and to represent Gayle as well. Good night, our sweet Charmaine.

Chapter 7:   How Do We Go On?

Those days after our families left seemed like empty days, with no purpose. But we had to keep going for Craig's sake. He was having difficulty with what had just happened to our family and his sister and best friend. Even our dog, Oliver, was affected by our loss. He had always been an easygoing dog, greeting friends and neighbors to our home with a wag of his tail. Now he was more of a watchdog, making sure no harm was going to come to the rest of his family. He would also go to Charmaine's room by himself and sit next to her bed with his chin resting on it. He did that for hours at a time for the rest of his life.

Craig spent many hours with our minister, who told us that he had never dealt with a child with such a strong need to understand what death was. He said Craig needed to understand why he could not be with Charmaine. That was the start of Craig's desire to experience death so he could be with her. At one point, Gayle went into Craig's room and he was halfway out his window, which was two stories up. That was his first attempt to take his life. Over the next twenty years, he would make that attempt over and over.

When Charmaine died of Reye's syndrome, it made the front page of our small-town newspaper. Charmaine was the first child in Washington State to die of this little-known disease. That year 135 children across the United States died of Reye's syndrome, a rare but serious condition that causes swelling in the liver and the brain. It most often affects young children and teenagers recovering from a viral infection, usually the flu or chicken pox, and it is believed to be an effect of taking aspirin. At the time, Reye's syndrome was always fatal.

We could feel people in town looking at us and keeping their distance. Aside from our family and a few friends, most people did not know what to say, or did not want to think about the fact that their own children could also die. Even some of my closest cousins pulled away from us. My employees and corporate leaders were a great support for me, however, and Gayle had friends and a sister who were very supportive. Especially helpful to us were our neighbor friend, Lucy, who helped with Craig when we were at the hospital, and her husband, Gene, who drove us from the first hospital to the second one when Charmaine was transferred there. Their family has remained close to us for forty years. Just recently, their youngest daughter, who was a good friend of Charmaine's, told Lucy that she is still learning from Charmaine.

Gayle's sister, Marsha, gave her first daughter the middle name Charmaine. When our niece was small, she asked her mother about the name, and Marsha told her about our Charmaine. The little girl responded that she'd known Charmaine when she herself was in heaven, before she was born.

Chapter 8:   Field of My Dreams

About a year after Charmaine's passing, I was in Portland on business, visiting a company that was set way back in a residential area—a strange place for a large building, in among all those houses. As I left this business one day, I was driving through the residential area and saw something from the corner of my eye. I continued driving for about a block and then for some reason decided to go back to that spot. As I pulled up to this field (which had no reason for being there, but there it was—a field full of beautiful wildflowers), I could see a young girl in a beautiful spring dress running through the flowers in the middle of the field. I watched her for a while, thinking, *That's what Charmaine would do.*

As I left, I felt a sense of love and relief: I now knew that Charmaine was in a happy place, just like in this field of my dreams. Whenever I went back to visit that business, I would try to find that field, but I never saw it again. I know now that my experience that day was a very special time in my life, a special time of remembering our Charmaine.

Chapter 9:   Craig and Sports

Because Craig was physically larger and stronger than other kids his age, with great coordination and eye-hand skills, we signed him up for baseball at an early age. I coached the team along with another father whose son was on the team. As co-coaches, we thought alike: we were never about the win; we were there to teach good sportsmanship and skills and to have fun. Those qualities just came naturally to the kids on this team. I think a lot of their success was due to fact that the parents had not pushed them into something they did not like.

Craig did well in baseball and the next year went on to play with the older kids. He had one problem, however: he could not stay in his position when playing the field. He was all over the place. Once when Gayle was in the stands, a woman asked her if all the boys had the number twelve on their shirts, because that was the only number she saw. Craig was number twelve. He eventually caught on that the other boys could actually play their own positions very well. Craig really enjoyed playing baseball, and we enjoyed watching him.

Craig also tried soccer, but it is a physical sport with a lot of body contact, and that set him off. The coach put him in as keeper, but it wasn't long before he became bored standing in the goal for long stretches of time. He started spending his time hanging upside down on the net. At one point he removed the net and walked off the field, saying, "This is boring."

The coached moved Craig to the field, but that didn't work out well either. It wasn't that other kids were knocking him around; it was that he was doing the knocking. During one game, the other team's parents were all over Craig for being too rough on their kids. The referee told the parents that what Craig was doing was well within the rules; it was just that the other kids did not play as hard as Craig did. Then a boy on the opposing team kicked the ball hard, straight into Craig's face, and laughed about it. He saw that Craig was mad and took off running. Craig chased the boy down and hit him in the face, giving him a bloody nose. At that point the opposing parents got so mad that they rushed the field and started pushing Craig around and hitting him. The referee tried to stop them, but he could not hold off five or six parents. I ran out on the field, grabbed Craig, and took him straight to the car. Some of the parents followed us all the way there, threatening me as well. That was the end of soccer.

As Craig was in a special needs class in school, he was invited to join a swim team for children with special needs. He would practice in the high school pool with the high school coach. I drove my van full of kids and one other adult to Olympia, Washington, for the state finals. Craig was in four different style races for his age group. He won all four. This was a sport that Craig could enjoy, and there was no body contact. The last event was for older boys who could do the four different strokes in one race. Craig was invited to participate as well. The event planners wanted to see if a younger boy could have the energy to last this race. Craig didn't just finish; he won. He was so proud, as was I.

After the meet, they had a dance for all the children. Four girls rode with us to Olympia, each with a different special need, and all four of them came over to me and asked me to dance with them. So I did. I danced with all four of them at the same time for several dances. It was one of the most enjoyable experiences I had had in a long time. I think it was also one of Craig's most enjoyable days. At these events, everybody was a winner, including the parents.

Chapter 10:   Gayle's Visit

One night while we were sleeping, something happened that I found both scary and surreal. Gayle has a very warm body temperature that I can feel when we are sleeping, even from some little ways away. But this night I awoke in the middle of the night and noticed a lack of warmth. I put my hand on Gayle and felt nothing but coolness. I pushed her a little and there was no response. I put my face directly in front of hers. She was not breathing. Even when I touched her face, there was nothing but cold—no reaction. I lay back and thought, *Oh my god—is she dead?* Yet my immediate thought was not to disturb her. If she was dead, she was with Charmaine. A few minutes later (it felt like an hour), I felt the warmth coming back into her body, and I could hear her breathing. I do not know why, but I did not disturb her during this time.

The next morning when we were in the kitchen, I asked her, "Where did you go last night?"

She wanted to know what I was talking about, and so I told her what I'd felt (or had not felt). She then told me that she'd been visiting with Charmaine, sitting in a rocking chair with Charmaine on her lap. It was the best feeling she had ever had, and she wanted to stay with Charmaine, but she knew she had to come back. Her life was not over, and there was more for her to do.

Like Gayle and me, Craig struggled with Charmaine's passing, although he expressed his grief with violent outrage. Our family doctor suggested taking him to a child psychiatrist. That was the beginning of a multitude of psychiatrists, therapists, and eventually hospitals.

Craig was angry at his mother for letting his sister die. I never understood why he felt this way toward Gayle and not me. At times he would attack her with knives and chairs. It was all Gayle could do to protect herself. One therapist taught her to wrap her arms around Craig, putting him face down on the floor with his hands and arms behind him, and stay on top of him until he calmed down. Sometimes she would have to do this for hours, once for five hours, before he calmed down. He would buck his head back so it hit Gayle in the face. After the five-hour hold-down, Gayle let him loose and told him that she knew he wanted to kill her but that she was not going to let that happen. Craig said that he knew he could, and he would.

His doctors tried several different medications, but none of them seemed to help. At one point our family was in therapy five days a week: some days it was just Craig, other days it was the three of us, and one day it was just Gayle and me.

As we had adopted Craig through a state adoption agency, we met with their social services representatives to see if there was any help they could provide. We asked for financial help as well as a recommendation for placement for Craig. They said that they could not place him anywhere. If we needed financial help, the only way they could provide it was if I was unemployed, we got a divorce, or we returned Craig to the adoption agency. These were not the answers we needed or wanted.

When Craig was eight, his psychiatrist sent him to the psychiatric ward of a children's hospital in Seattle. He was there for six weeks. They diagnosed him as bipolar, hyperactive, and psychotic, but they also said he was highly intelligent. They recommended that he be put in a residential facility. Unfortunately, the adoption service would not help with the cost, and we could not afford it on our own.

So Craig came home and our lives remained the same. It was a tough choice to keep him at home when he was so violent, especially toward Gayle, but returning him to the adoption service to be put in foster care did not seem like a good option. I felt that he needed love and support.

Little did I know how difficult having Craig home would be, especially for Gayle. I worried that she could not take much more of his violence. I would come home from work some days and not know if she was still going to be there. Many times when I got home, she would leave just to separate herself from all that violence. Thank God she always returned.

I felt that one of the reasons Gayle always returned was our dog, Oliver, who was one of the true blessings of our family. Because he was a mix of Norwegian elkhound and standard poodle, he looked like an elkhound with a bad perm. He was the most easygoing dog I had ever known. But he was also the one thing Gayle could always count on for security when Craig was so dangerous.

A year or so after Charmaine's passing, Oliver began experiencing prolonged bouts of illness, and I had to take him to the vet several times. Finally, the vet asked to keep him overnight for observation. The vet called me at work the next day and told me that Oliver was in a coma and was not expected to survive. I stopped by the vet's office on my way home to sign the papers to have Oliver put to rest. I asked the vet to do it then, so I could go home and tell Gayle and Craig that Oliver was dead. He said he would do it as soon as I left. I went home and broke the bad news. We all were very sad, and there were a lot of tears that night.

The next morning, we got a call from the vet. He said that he'd had to attend to an emergency delivery with a horse as soon as I left the vet's office. When he came back to take care of Oliver, there he was, sitting up in the kennel. He seemed perfectly fine. Would we like to come and visit him?

We rushed to the vets to find Oliver still doing well. We were overjoyed, having spent the night in tears over losing him. Craig was especially overjoyed, because he had been especially upset that he had not gotten to say good-bye to his dog—the same thing that had happened with his sister. Craig sat down with Oliver and enjoyed some time with Oliver on his lap.

The vet wanted to keep Oliver one more day just to make sure he was fine. He called us later to say that he had been sitting down with Oliver on his lap when Oliver just stopped breathing. So we went through a second day of losing Oliver, but we now knew that he was with Charmaine.

At this point Craig was still in public school, in a special needs class. His teacher and the teacher assistant were very patient with him and worked hard to keep him from hurting other children or himself.

Not every day was totally bad for Craig. Sometimes he seemed almost as normal as other children. One funny story about Craig happened at school. The special needs class had several grade levels in the same classroom. During recess, he met an older girl, a student in the regular class, and they became friends. Then one day Craig came home and told Gayle, "I will never do that again." When she asked him what he meant, he said, "I will never tell another girl my age." Apparently, this girl he liked had asked his age, and when he told her he was eight, she walked away and would not talk to him again. Craig said that she was ten years old. She'd apparently thought that he was her age.

By now Craig had become a real con artist, and he could "turn on" an act like a normal child. He also could convince people who did not know him to do all sorts of things. One day we hired a neighbor girl to babysit Craig just for a few hours during the day. Her parents were two houses away and said they would keep an eye on them. Craig had some trick handcuffs that would fall off very easily. He was playing with the babysitter in his room and convinced her to let him handcuff her after showing her how easily they came off. He handcuffed her to the bed I had made, which was very strong. He did something to the handcuffs so they would not unlock, and she stayed locked up for more than an hour. When we came home, Craig was out in the street by himself. We went into the house and found the babysitter cuffed to the bed, crying. We let her loose, and that was the last time she spoke to him or us. That was also the end of the handcuffs.

The violence continued to get worse. Craig was bullied in school for being in a special needs class, but the bullying stopped after Craig hit one of the kids so hard that he fell and hit his head. The boy was in the hospital for days. Craig's teacher said the boy had provoked Craig and would not let up until Craig had had enough. The boy was ultimately fine, but the incident made us scared about what could happen in the future. We never understood why the teacher let the other boy continue to taunt Craig.

Chapter 11: Mount St. Helens

The house we built on a hill had a beautiful view of the top of Mount St. Helens. It was something that was very special to us. When we first moved to Longview, Mount St. Helens and Spirit Lake were the places to go for family enjoyment and solitude.

On May 18, 1980, we were in church, waiting for the service to be over so we could start the church picnic, when somebody came in and said, "The mountain has exploded!" We were told that we should all go home and stay inside.

When we got home and looked out our living room window at the mountain, we were devastated to see what was going on. We watched it, along with the news coverage, for hours.

The Cowlitz River was just a quarter mile down the hill from our home. The news kept saying that there was the possibility of floods coming our way. I was not too concerned, because our house was built about a hundred feet above the river level.

Later in the day, we walked down to the river to see what was happening. I wish now that we had never gone. Everything imaginable was floating down the river, from houses and cars to wild animals and every kind of debris possible. We didn't stay long before heading home. The ash plume was moving to the east, the opposite direction from where we lived.

A few days later, the schools were still closed, as was most of the town. Craig was not handling this devastation very well, and so we decided to leave for California to stay at Gayle's parents' home on Catalina Island. They were gone, and we had the house to ourselves. After the following weekend, when the ash turned to the west, I called work and was told by my employees that it was pitch-black in the middle of the day because of the ash. I told them that they should be home with their families.

Craig was doing better, and so we returned home about ten days later, only to find everything covered in ash. We moved from Longview in 1983 to West Linn, just south of Portland.

Chapter 12: My Turning Point

Gayle's days with Craig were getting worse and worse. I was having a lot of difficulties with him as well. He was getting so strong that I had a hard time holding him down when he was out of control.

Gayle and I talked it over, and we thought it would be a good idea for her to get away for a while. She called her sister, who lived on Catalina Island, to see if the two of them could spend time together away from family. They decided to go to Santa Barbara for a few days and then to a fun park, and also to visit their brother and his family in San Diego. It was all set: I would take some vacation time and stay home with Craig.

Gayle seemed happy as we took her to the airport in Portland. We agreed that there was no need for phone calls during her time away unless there was an emergency. Off she went!

I was amazed by how well Craig did the first few days. We stayed around the house, and I did some landscaping that needed to be done.

Craig knew that Gayle and her sister were going to a fun park at some point during their time together in Southern California, and he kept saying that he would like to go there with me. I fell right into his con game. I agreed that we could drive down and spend a day at the fun park and Gayle would not even know we were there. We would tell her when she came home. I did not know what day she and her sister were planning to be there.

Off we went for a two-day drive. Craig was relatively well behaved during that time. We arrived at the fun park and rode lots of rides and had a great time together.

As we were walking to another area of the park, there were Gayle and her sister, walking toward us. I knew the second I saw the expression on Gayle's face that this was the worst possible thing that I could have done to her. She did not even look happy to see us, or say she was happy. It was the most terrible thing that could have happened to her while she was trying to enjoy some time with Marsha and away from Craig. I honestly don't remember the rest of that day. I just knew that I had made a gigantic mistake by taking Craig to where Gayle was.

I am not sure how it was decided that Marsha would go back to Catalina Island to be with her family while the three of us went down to San Diego to visit Gayle's brother, his wife, and their teenage son, Rob.

That evening Rob slept over with a friend so there would be more room for us. Gayle and I slept in his room, and Craig slept in the den. The next day when Rob came home, he realized that he was missing the money from his paycheck, which he just cashed, and some silver dollars. I immediately asked Craig if he knew anything about it. Of course, he said he did not know anything. I went and checked Craig's suitcase and found it all.

Gayle and I were devastated that Craig would do something like this to his cousin. After offering our deepest apologies, we left for home. Gayle still had a ticket to fly home, but she decided to drive with us. I think she was worried about me because I was so distraught. I believe that this was when I knew that we would have to do something with Craig. This was one of the lowest points of my life concerning our son.

On the drive home I did not speak at all. In fact, I started crying. Between Craig's actions—conning me to go to the fun park and then stealing from his cousin—and my knowledge that I'd disappointed Gayle so much by showing up when she was having such a good time, it all began piling up on me and I just fell apart.

Gayle was worried about me driving, but I continued somehow. It was all such a blur. It seemed that I was sobbing throughout the long drive to Redding, California, where we stopped for the night. The next morning while we were eating breakfast at the hotel restaurant, Craig got really out of sorts and mad, and he stormed off, leaving us in the restaurant. I told Gayle that if he was not back by the time we were ready to leave, we should just leave without him. That's how much I was hurting. I know that I would not have left our ten-year-old son, but that is how I felt. On the way back to our room, we ran into Craig. The three of us left shortly after that.

I was in such a state that I don't remember anything about driving home. I look back at this time, which I rarely mention to anybody, and can see that I was having some kind of breakdown. It was so much for me to handle. I now understand some of what Gayle went through for so many years with Craig.

I had always hoped to be able to take care of Craig somehow. As adoptive parents, we felt that he should be treated and cared for no differently than our biological child. But we were facing choices I could not comprehend. The social worker had told us our only options if we wanted to receive their help were for me to quit my job and be on welfare, for me to leave Gayle so she would be on welfare, or for us to give Craig back to them and have nothing to do with him again, and then he would go into the foster care system. At the time, we had not gone with any of those options. But should we now?

We'd had enough, and we did not know how we could continue as a family. Craig's psychiatrist had him placed back in the hospital psychiatric ward in Seattle. He was there for another six weeks.

We met with the head of the ward each Friday, and if Craig was able to go with us, we would take him for the day on Saturday. That did not always work, and sometimes we had him for only a short time. It all depended on his ability to stay calm.

During one visit, the head of the ward told us that he'd gone into a viewing closet to watch the floor activity through a one-way mirror. When he was finished, he met with the staff and asked them who was in charge of the floor. One staff member answered that it was her duty as head nurse to be in charge. He said, "No, Craig was in charge." Craig had the whole staff doing exactly what he wanted then to do, and they did not know how that was happening. Craig had complete control of the ward.

After the six weeks was up, the head of children's psychiatric ward once again told us that for Craig's safety and the safety of others around him, he would need to be in a care facility. He recommended a facility in Seattle. Once again, we told him we could not afford it. He told us to leave and not come back; he would contact the state adoption agency and force them to pay for Craig's care. I felt this was child abandonment, but he said he would take care of it.

Once the agency agreed to pay for a portion (we would have to pay the rest), Craig was ready to be moved. Gayle and I asked that we be the ones to move him to his new home. There were only a few miles between the two facilities. And so we picked up Craig and his belongings and transported him, explaining as well as we could where he was going to be living and that we would visit him every week.

We had not visited the care facility prior to taking Craig there. Once we arrived, we could see that it was the right place for him.

As we left him there, our hearts felt sad for what we had done to Craig, but we realized later that it was what we had done *for* Craig. His care had been our priority for his whole life. This was a positive move for Craig's health and for our sanity. When we returned home, it was as if a thousand pounds had been lifted off us.

This was not the end of our care and love for Craig, but it was the start of recovery for all three of us.

The staff wanted to get Craig settled in for a few weeks before we visited him and met his personal staff. Craig had the ability to con even the best of their educated staff members. When we arrived to visit Craig and meet with his therapist, we realized what awful parents we were, according to Craig and his therapist. Once again, Craig had worked his best con act. It would not do any good to try to convince the staff of anything different. We just needed to give them more time to find out the truth for themselves.

A few weeks later, we were in a room with Craig and his therapist. This room had a ten-foot-long, heavy wooden table. Remember that Craig at the age of ten had the strength of a grown man. At one point he lost it and pushed this very large table and the three of us against the wall, yelling that he was going to kill us and the therapist. They finally got Craig under control, and we left.

One time we were invited to come to the facility for a parents' spaghetti dinner with the children and staff. Upon arriving, we were told that Craig had run away, and that this was not the first time. We left and had dinner by ourselves.

One of the times that Craig ran away, he made it to Lake Union, hot-wired a sailboat, and took it through the locks, convincing the lock staff that his father was just below, in the boat, and that he had taken it through the locks many times prior. The authorities found him out to sea in the Puget Sound. Craig told them he was headed to Tahiti.

During his stay at this facility, Craig was supposed to get a school education as well as being cared for and receiving therapy. That was the plan, but Craig was so difficult that they decided it was better to keep him out of class so the other children could learn.

One day we received a call from the facility letting us know that we should not come for our weekly visit. Craig had locked himself and another boy in their second-floor room, saying that he wanted to talk to the governor about better food and conditions. After trying several times to get into the room, the staff finally gave up. They figured Craig could not hurt himself or anybody else, so they left him there to come out when he got hungry. But Craig would wait until nighttime and sneak into the kitchen to get all the food the two of them could eat. Several days went by, and the firefighters finally broke down the door after Craig started a fire in the room. The care facility had a hard time keeping staff members after they'd dealt with Craig for long periods of time.

Chapter 13: Good Times

While Craig was still in the Seattle care facility, I would pick him up now and then to take him camping. One time I picked up one of Craig's neighborhood friends to go camping with us. Craig did not have many friends. This one seemed to understand Craig, and Craig liked being with him. We camped at Lake Cushman on the Olympic mountain range. I pretty much let them do what they wanted to do. It was their time, and I thought they would enjoy having a little independence, although I was always present and part of what they were doing.

Next to our campsite was a family that had several children with them. One was hearing impaired, and the whole family would sign with him to communicate. At one point Craig went over there to visit them, and I saw him signing with the boy. I could not believe that Craig knew how to sign. When he came back to our camp, I asked him how he'd learned to sign. He said that when he was in the children's hospital, he was roommates with a boy who was hearing impaired, and that was the only way the two of them could communicate. He was a fast learner.

We also took Craig to a Neal Diamond concert in Seattle. He had the greatest of times, and he still talks about that concert to this day. When we had good times with Craig, he was a joy to be with. Unfortunately, they did not last for very long before he reverted back to being difficult. But those times always gave us hope that someday we could all live in peace.

When Craig was moved to the care facility at age ten, the state adoption agency paid part of the cost for him to stay there, and we paid the balance. That was the arrangement until he turned eighteen. It did not matter where he was staying; the cost continued. We could not afford the full amount that the agency told us we had to pay each month, and so even after Craig was released at age eighteen, we continued to put money toward the balance until it was paid in full.

Gayle and I went to court every six months for those eight years. The state appointed an attorney to represent Craig in court, although she never met Craig or interviewed him on the phone. She did not even communicate with the facilities Craig lived in. She would just meet with us for a few minutes before we met with the judge, and then she would act like she had communicated with the facility staff. The meeting was handled in such a way that the attorney never said that she had not met Craig or talked to anyone from whatever facility he was in at the time. We would have to bring all our financial information for the judge to review, and every six months the judge would increase our share of the cost for Craig's care, even though it was clear that we could not afford that much. We had no choice. Craig was being cared for, and we would meet with him as often as his situation allowed.

We continued to live in the house we had built for our family, and with so much of it having been designed for Charmaine and Craig, it was difficult and painful to be reminded of them both as we tried to continue our relationship with Craig. We had heard that 85 percent of all marriages fail after the loss of a child—and in many ways we had lost two children, although we still had a relationship with Craig and continued to love him no matter the circumstances. In the seventies there were not organizations that helped parents who had lost a child.

It was also difficult living in Longview, having lost so many friends after Charmaine's death and Craig's issues. Every day, and everywhere we went, there were reminders and stares.

The company that I worked for was very supportive of me during those difficult years. I had a sales staff in Seattle, and I would go there most Fridays and take Gayle with me. I would work in the morning and then we would spend the afternoon at the care facility, meeting with the staff and Craig. If Craig was doing well, we would take him on Saturday to visit various places we thought he would enjoy. Not all Saturdays worked out. Some of our visits lasted hours, and some lasted just minutes before we would have to take him back. We got a new puppy and started bringing her with us to see him. Craig really liked the puppy, and they played together a lot.

One night we took Craig out to dinner in Seattle, and while we were eating, a *very* large man came to the table and in a very deep voice said, "Hello, Craig." We were afraid that this was somebody Craig had offended somehow. It ended up being a member of the Seahawks football team. The man told us that several members of the team regularly went to the care facility to play football with the kids. Several of them liked to play with Craig because he was so strong. We thought that it was very nice of them to do that, and to remember Craig—although the man scared us in the beginning.

Soon after that, the owner of a Portland company, someone I had known for several years, approached me to take over its management. That would mean selling our house and moving to the Portland area. We decided that this might be the best thing for us.

It took two years to sell our house because it was so close to the flood zone after Mount St. Helen's erupted. I took the job and commuted fifty miles each way for those two years. But it was worth it.

Chapter 14: Craig Is Moving On

After more than two years in the care facility in Seattle, the staff needed Craig to move to another facility. They had lost several staff members who just could not deal with working with him. This new facility was on an island, and it housed around a dozen boys who were challenged by one issue or another. The only thing on this island was the facility. It had an office in a town on the mainland where we would go to meet with Craig and the staff. They would boat Craig from the facility to the town to meet with us. Sometimes we were able to take him for a few hours, but we would have to be back in time for him to catch the return boat. Our visits were becoming fewer and fewer, but that was not by our choice. The staff would not let Craig have many visits because of his behavior. We also were never allowed to visit the facility on the island.

We did find out that the facility's doctor had given Craig medication to see if it would keep him on a more stable level. They told us that the doctor had increased the medication a little at a time until the highest recommended level was reached. It had little to no effect on Craig. In their opinion, the only thing they could do was keep him safe from others and himself.

Craig was held on this island for several years. The agency tried foster care a few times, but that did not last more than a few weeks. Before Craig turned eighteen, he was moved to a work group facility in Oregon. He had mentioned that he was training to be a welder and then had taken culinary classes. He called to tell us that if he finished the classes, the facility would help him find a cooking job on a cruise ship. He ended his time there when they kicked him out for selling drugs.

When Craig turned eighteen, the agency released him to fend for himself. They contacted us to see if we could help him get settled.

I was aware of a facility in Longview, Washington, the town where Craig lived until he was ten. I arranged and paid to have him stay at this facility. The rule for staying there was that he would have to find work and keep it for the month that we had paid for him. From our years of living in Longview, I had several friends there who owned businesses and were kind enough to offer him work. We later found out that Craig started and left five different jobs in a single week. He eventually worked ringing a bell and collecting donations, as it was the holiday season.

At the end of the month, a member of the management at the facility where Craig was living called me to see if I was going to pay for another month. Craig had not worked very much during that first month, and the staff member said that Craig had told them to call me and I would pay for him. It was one of the hardest things I've ever done, but I said no. Craig needed to carry some of the load himself.

Months went by without a word from Craig. He fled Longview because his drug dealer was looking to harm him, and he later told us that he hitchhiked to Seattle, where he lived on the streets or in flophouses. Drugs where his downfall; self-medicating was the only way he felt he could survive. We really did not know what he was doing for months or even years at a time. From time to time we would get calls from the Seattle police saying that he was in jail.

Our hearts were broken during those years of knowing what kind of life he was living, or not living. I was often in Seattle on business, and I always worried that I might see him when I was driving in the kind of neighborhood where he was probably living.

I never did see him, thank God. I don't know which I would have done—turned the other way or tried to help him. I knew that he was the only one that could help himself. At that time, drugs were what ran his life. At one point he called me to see if we could get together. I agreed, and I found the halfway house where he was living at the time. All the clothes passed out to the people staying there were hand-me-downs. I took Craig to a store and bought him a few full sets of clothes to help him get through the winter.

One time we received a phone call from the police telling us that Craig was in jail and had tried to cut his wrist with a tooth-brush he'd sharpened on the concrete floor of his cell. We heard these kinds of stories for years.

Craig did share with us that he had signed up to work on a fishing boat in Alaska. During his first trip he worked as a cook's assistant, and the next trip he would be working in the boat's freezer. He did not need to tell us how hard those jobs were. We had seen television programs that showed how tough the work was on those boats. We hoped that working on those fishing boats would keep him away from drugs.

Chapter 15: Was This the End?

Months and months went by without any communication from Craig. He was an adult now, and we had no way of finding him. Even if we did, our interference was not going to change anything.

Eventually we received the call that we never wanted to get but knew we would get at some point. A hospital staffer called to tell us that Craig had been injected in his neck with cocaine. They had resuscitated him three times that day, and they did not know if he was going to live or die. Once again in our long years of not knowing what was happening to him, we couldn't do anything but pray. We asked the person who called if he would notify us if Craig did die; we would follow up with whatever it would take to see that he had a proper burial.

When Charmaine passed, we'd purchased three additional plots around hers. To this day, we still own them. Thank God we did not have to use one of them for Craig.

We never heard back from the hospital. Not knowing was destroying us. Knowing what your child is going through is horrible, but not knowing anything of what his life is like is almost the same as knowing that he is dead. In some ways, death sounded more peaceful than what he was going through.

Several days after the call from the hospital, we received a call from a minister who ran a Christian program for men who needed some help, prayers, and guidance. He told us that a male nurse had gone into Craig's hospital room after the third time they resuscitated him. This nurse (we refer to him as "Craig's guiding angel") told Craig that this was his last chance to live. If Craig wanted to continue to live, and if he was willing to change his lifestyle, the nurse would take him somewhere that could help him—it was his choice. We've thanked God over and over again that Craig chose to live.

We were told that this facility was supported by several local churches in the community. As part of the conditions for staying there, Craig would have to work for different church members, doing whatever was necessary. He would also have to stay clean of drugs or he would be asked to leave.

We went up to visit Craig after he'd had time to get settled in his new environment. We met with the minister, who seemed to have taken particular interest in Craig. He said that Craig was doing well. He was working when people needed help with manual labor. He was also attending church as part of his agreement to stay there.

We also had a chance to visit with Craig. It was such a relief to see him, especially because he seemed to be doing well. It had been a very long time since I hugged him. God willing, this would be a turn in his life. Gayle still had a hard time hugging him because he had hurt her so badly.

At times when Craig was working for people, they would have him stay overnight so he could continue to work early the next day. We found out that sometimes he slept in a chicken coop. That did not seem to bother him. It was probably better than sleeping on the streets of Seattle.

He was doing really well as far as we knew, so I thought I would pick him up and take him camping. He was staying with a family at the time, and the man was a builder; he had Craig helping build pole buildings. When I arrived at their home to pick up Craig, they were very nice to me and seemed to really like him. Craig was proud to show me his living quarters: several sheets of plywood laid across the rafters in their garage, and a mattress and blankets. We did go camping, and it was a joy for me to spend time with our son after all those years of concern and worries. Gayle did not like to camp, and so she did not go on that visit, but she did go along on other visits with Craig. She was very guarded after all his attempts on her life.

Over a period of time, Craig did some painting for several people connected with the churches that supported the mission. He even got to the point that he was doing work on his own. Then he was able to buy a truck and some equipment. He was a very hard worker, and the people he worked for really liked him. He rented a small apartment that was part of a garage.

Then we invited Craig to come to our home for some weekend visits. For the most part they were enjoyable. One weekend we invited him to come for a barbeque. We had a large backyard, and I would set up the croquet set to play. I was barbequing some ribs while we played, and pretty soon they were smoking heavily. We stopped playing, and I checked them: they were burned to a crisp. We all had a big laugh, especially Craig, because Dad never made mistakes. We ended up eating leftover Chinese food.

Somehow with God's help, Craig had made it through some of the toughest years of his and our lives. When we saw him, he always seemed to be clean of drugs and happy with his life. He had always made friends easily. Times were good, and we really enjoyed being around him. He was proud of himself and his accomplishments, as were we.

One day we got a call from Craig, asking us if we would like to come to his wedding.

What? We did not even know he was seeing anybody. Come to find out, she was the daughter of the minister who had helped turn his life around. They were getting married the next weekend. We offered to host the rehearsal dinner the night before the weeding. They lived about an hour north of Seattle, and so it would be a two- or three-day trip. Gayle's niece was living in Portland at the time—she knew Craig a little—and she wanted to go as well. Gene and Lucy, our friends who helped us so much over the years with Charmaine and Craig, also wanted to go to the wedding. There were no invitations or showers.

We found the church where they were going to get married and met his wife-to-be and her mother. We had already talked to her father several times at his mission.

Craig had made reservations at a Greek restaurant with a private dining room. There were about twenty-five family and friends there altogether. The only ones we knew were Craig and the bride's father.

The next day when we arrived at the church, Craig was standing out front in a tuxedo. We almost did not recognize him. He was never one to get dressed up or even comb his hair. One of my favorite pictures of Craig is of the two of us waiting in front of the church, joking around and laughing. Gayle is in the background, also laughing, but you can't see her very well. It would have been nice to have her in the picture too, but it was one of those spur-of-the-moment shots. The wedding was beautiful. We were so proud of Craig and his new wife. There was a reception organized by the ladies at the church.

Gayle and I rented a house on one of the San Juan Islands for their honeymoon. It was a beautiful setting, and they really enjoyed it, especially having breakfast delivered to their house each day.

Chapter 16: Craig's Better Life

Craig seemed to have his life in order. He was married, he owned his own painting business, and he and his wife were very happy. It was not too long before they bought a house and fixed it up, and it was not too much longer before they were expecting a baby. We would visit them on occasion, and Craig was always proud to show us their home and all the work they had done to make it their own. They even got a dog. When we visited, Craig and I would spend a lot of time throwing the ball for their dog. I taught Craig how to barbeque (and how not to burn the ribs). Craig did not seem to be using drugs during this time, but it was hard for us to detect these things. We really don't think he was using during those years. We were very proud of him for that.

One day in July, we got the call from Craig that his wife was going into the hospital to have their baby. By time we got there, she'd had a baby boy. I still have a picture on my desk of Gayle holding our very own grandson. One of God's miracles: we were grandparents, something we never thought would happen. God had blessed us all.

Several months later, we all went on a short vacation to a resort in Bend, Oregon. We shared a rented house that would hold us all. They also brought their dog. Craig loved throwing sticks into the river for their dog to retrieve. We rented canoes and paddled up and down the river.

Craig's wife and I talked about horses that we could rent. Neither of us had ridden horses much, only as kids. We did not want to go on one of those horse rides where everybody is in a line, going very slowly. When we went to the rental stalls and asked if we could run the horses, they said they had a guide who would let us run them if we were qualified to do so. We both said we were. So just the two of us and the guide headed out, very slowly to begin with. Then the guide said, "Let's do it!" and she took off and the two of us followed. We were going pretty fast and not riding very well, but we held on. After a while we stopped, and the guide asked, "You have never ridden a horse at full gallop, have you?" We were caught, but the guide said, "Let's keep going." I was so glad we had a hot tub waiting for us back at the house. Gayle and Craig laughed at us the rest of the night. This was the first time in Craig's thirty-plus years that we had enjoyed being with him for several days at a time. We had always had some times when things went well, but not like this one. How wonderful! We felt God's blessings.

For a few years we would visit Craig and his family fairly regularly. They seemed happy and seemed to be progressing just like any other family. Often we would grill some steaks. Craig bought a grill, but he did not know how to use it very well. I would provide instruction as we cooked.

They purchased another house in their neighborhood with the intention of renting it out. Craig's business was going strong. He had several trucks fully equipped for the painting business. They purchased a new Volvo just like the one Gayle and I had for many years. He also purchased a really nice pickup truck for himself.

Chapter 17: Craig Tumbles

One day Craig called us, very distraught, and the conversation was nothing but bad news. He and his wife had split up. He'd moved out and left the house to his wife and son. It seemed to us that he had started back on drugs. We did not know much about their situation other than when he walked away, he left everything in his wife's hands. It was not long before they had lost everything, including his business and all the equipment. For quite some time, we did not know what he was doing or anything about his wife and our grandson.

They did divorce, and Craig was once again using drugs for some time. One day he contacted us and said that he wanted to get back into business but did not have the funds. We wanted to help, but not knowing if he was on drugs, we did not want to give him cash. As we had been wanting to get the inside of our house painted for some time, we offered to buy the basic equipment that he would need to come to our home and paint the interior. He would also need a van for his business. I gave him my brother's phone number so he could ask him if he would also help. He did, and they worked out a deal for Craig to pay him back over a period of time. I was very happy that my brother was willing to give Craig a chance. My nephew also helped him out.

He did come to our house, and he seemed to be clean of drugs. I took him to the paint store to buy what he needed to get started and paint our place. He did a wonderful job. I could see why he had been so successful; he was one of the most personable people I had ever met—both funny and intelligent. I had the opportunity to watch him introduce himself to the owner of a large hotel out on the coast. He was very professional and honest and made the owner feel like he would be a good person to work with. Craig got the project, and he and his crew did such a great job that the owner had other hotels that he wanted him to handle.

Craig moved to Bellingham, Washington, and started a business in that area. He had his son on the weekends. The two of them really liked this area near the Puget Sound.

Then Craig met a woman who had two teenage daughters. She rented a beautiful house on a lake, and Craig invited us up to meet her and her daughters. They were a very nice family.

Soon after that, he called us to say that they were standing on the end of the dock and had just gotten married. Another surprise. They moved to a different house that could hold the whole family. Their marriage did not last long.

We learned that Craig started attending a twelve-step program in the area. We were so happy for him and proud that he had made a comeback from such difficult times.

Craig is someone who can carry on a conversation with anybody. He has a real talent for making friends. One day he was working on a house in Birch Bay, just north of Bellingham, when he began talking to the man across the street from where he was working. This man told him that he and his wife were building a cabin in the mountains, and they wanted to sell their house with them holding the contract. This was a great opportunity for Craig, as he would avoid dealing with the bank and credit checks. They agreed on a price, and Craig and his son moved in. The house was livable, but Craig wanted to make it his own. Over several years he has made this house into a really nice home of which we all are so proud.

The last four or five years have been the best years ever with Craig. He has found somebody new and they have a wonderful relationship. We really like her and enjoy the two of them whenever we get together. Craig's son is doing well and really likes living in their home and the neighborhood, which sits on a bay. When Craig first moved there, he would call me very early in the morning and tell me that he was sitting on a log next to the bay and watching the bald eagles fishing for their breakfast. Then he would tell me that the sun was coming up behind the mountains and that it was just beautiful. I would say to him, "Who is this?" and we would laugh because we both knew that this was not the way our lives had functioned in the past.

I have never been so proud of Craig, the life he has made for himself and his family, and our relationship. He has worked very hard to become the person he is now. God has blessed us all.

Craig knows that his mother loves flowers, as she was a floral designer for eleven years. So he orders absolutely beautiful flower arrangements and has them delivered to her—sometimes for special occasions, but often just to let her know that he loves her. He will also send me a package of frozen fish—not just any fish, but the kind of fish he knows I enjoy. Many times it will be a mix of several different items like salmon, catfish, sole, frog legs, alligator, and crayfish.

Craig has been very involved with a twelve-step program for several years now, and we know it has helped him stay clean. He is even a sponsor for some new members. He has a sponsor as well. One day Craig called and said that he and his sponsor wanted to pay us a visit. One of the twelve steps (the ninth) requires you to confront people you have hurt, and so they wanted to come to our house for a few hours. We live about five hours away from him. They drove down, spent several hours with us, and drove straight back. I have done that at times, to pick up our grandson and bring him to our home for several days. It is a tough haul.

Gayle and I were apprehensive about this meeting. We were not sure how much we should share about the life we lived during those thirty-plus years. Craig's sponsor, Don, was really good at knowing how to start the conversation between Craig and us. We did share a lot of the hurt that Craig had caused in our family and even in some of our friendships, and we talked about how difficult it was for us not knowing what his life was like when he was so involved with drugs and living on the streets. He shared a lot of his life experiences and expressed regret for the pain he had put us through. We also described our feelings when we were able to enjoy Craig. There were times that he was very fun to be around, but we always had to be on guard, not knowing when he would react violently.

Before we finished, Craig's sponsor expressed his feelings about Gayle and me, saying how amazing it was that we'd helped Craig through some of the toughest of all possible times.

We all hugged and said how much we loved each other.

Craig is one of the funniest people we know. He is also very intelligent and knows most of what is going on in the world. Craig and his family have become very big fans of the Seahawks football team. They have team shirts, and he texts me during games to tell me what is happening with their team. I do not care much for football, but it is a joy to hear how much they enjoy it as a family.

Chapter 18 The Time of Our Lives

Craig called me one day and asked if I would like to join him and his son on a trip to a California fun park. That's something that I never thought would happen with our son, let alone with our grandson. There was no hesitation in my answer.

They flew from Bellingham, I flew from Portland, and we met in Los Angeles. I was excited that I would have a chance to take them both to Gardena, the community where Gayle and I lived when we were kids. I wanted to show them the houses where we grew up and where we lived when we first got married, plus the best thing in Gardena, the Italian deli downtown that was our favorite from our early years. The deli was still in business and as popular as ever, but we arrived five minutes after it had closed for the day. Disappointed but not discouraged, we decided to come back on the way to the airport going home.

How great it was to be with our eight-year-old grandson—and with our son, who seemed to be the same age as *his* son when it came to their level of excitement. I'd grown up going to this fun park, starting with my first time the second week it was open. Gayle and I had taken Charmaine there from as early an age as possible. She loved all the rides, especially the ones for younger children. I loved riding them with her just to see her face and her enjoyment. Our last visit there with her was on her eighth birthday. The picture on the back cover of this book is a painting of a photograph that was taken that day, just four months prior to her death. Craig was with us that last visit with Charmaine. She loved showing the fun park to him. They both had the time of their lives.

I never thought I would reach the age where I would refuse to ride certain rides, but that is the case now. Craig and his son rode each and every ride that would have given me a heart attack or a neck injury. It was fun to see and hear their excitement.

The three of us took an extra day and rode the ferry over to Catalina to visit Gayle's family. It was the first time that Craig's son got to meet his great-grandmother. What a wonderful time we all had visiting and sharing about our time in California.

After all the tough years with Craig and his struggles, just seeing him and his son living what most people think of as a normal part of life was like winning the lottery to me.

Chapter 19: Gayle's Stroke

Around 1990, Gayle took a job as a floral designer. It was during a time that was very tough for me as the income provider for our family. Gayle had not worked full-time since we first married. For many years she did seamstress work, designing and sewing wedding dresses for daughters of friends of ours. She really loved doing this, and it made her feel proud when we would go to a wedding and so many people would praise her work.

Now Gayle was working a full schedule doing floral design at a local store. She loved designing, and working with people who appreciated her talents. Often clients came to her to buy flowers for someone who was going through difficult times. Gayle is a good listener and very compassionate. I always felt her job was as therapeutic for her as it was financially helpful to us.

One day she tripped on a floor mat and fell straight down on her knees, traumatizing her neck. She had to wear a neck brace and was out of work for several weeks. During that time, I noticed a few oddities about her. She complained about her eyesight not being what it had been. She went to the doctor, but he could not find anything wrong with her eyes. Her sight continued to get worse, so one Friday she was sent to a specialist. He did extensive tests and did not find anything wrong with her eyes or the nerves going from the eyes to the brain. He suggested that she come back on Monday for more evaluations.

As the next day was Saturday, I decided to get her out of the house for a while. We took a short ride in the hills around our home, and then I stopped to look at some horses that were close to the fence next to the road. Gayle said that she could not make out that they were horses. She said they looked like something you would see through half-frozen water in a clear glass bowl.

That scared me enough to go straight home. We had a neighbor who was a legal aid for an attorney who dealt primarily with medical cases. Upon telling her about Gayle's vision problem, she said, "Get her to the hospital *now*." She thought Gayle was having a stroke.

We went straight to the hospital, where, after several tests, they confirmed that a number of blood clots had worked their way into Gayle's brain. They put her on some medications and kept her in the hospital for a few days.

The doctor told me that she would have some difficulty from these blood clots. Due to her fall, one of the arteries to her brain was traumatized and plugged. Some of the blood, in the form of clots, had broken loose and gone into her brain. The doctors were able to dissolve these with medication. She would have to be on a blood thinner for the rest of her life.

Gayle has three distinct medical restrictions, but they do not affect her day-to-day functions. The doctor did tell me that if I had not brought her to the hospital when I did, she would most likely not have made it through the next day. Thank you, God, and we thank our neighbor.

Chapter 20: Music to Our Ears

Music has always been a big part of Gayle's life. When she was a child, she preferred playing her records over watching television. In the early days of our marriage, we went to several live concerts in the Los Angeles area, where we had grown up and lived the first five years of our marriage. Our choice of music was not the rock and roll of the day. We both enjoyed Big Band music and singers like Ella Fitzgerald.

For many years after we moved to the Northwest, we attended very few live performances. Once smoking was banned in public places, we were able to go to some of the small jazz clubs for dinner and entertainment. We tried a Neil Diamond concert once—and got hooked. We even took Craig to a Neil Diamond concert in Seattle when Craig was living in a care facility. He really loved it because it was loud and active entertainment. He still talks about that concert. So do we, because it was one of those rare times when all our family members enjoyed each other for an entire evening.

It was those kinds of times that helped keep our family together. With so much of Craig's life having been a struggle for all of us, any time we had a day—or even part of a day—when things jelled, it gave us hope and the strength to keep trying to bring our family back to what it should be: an abundance of love and mutual respect.

A friend of mine who recently lost his daughter to cancer asked me how it was possible that Gayle and I held our marriage together after our daughter died. I replied, "We both believe that Charmaine's spirit always stays close to us, and we would not want to disappoint her with anything we do in our lives or by how we treat each other."

Now Craig and his family regularly attend concerts in their area. It is a tradition Gayle and I feel we passed on to him, and it stuck. Often when Craig and his family come to visit, we will take them to our favorite entertainment club, Tony Starlight's, where the owner is also one of the main entertainers. He performs and sings as many of the great signers of the past, including Louis Armstrong and Neil Diamond. We have attended his Neil Diamond nights more than a half dozen times. Each time we go, we're reminded of the wonderful evening we had with Craig so many years ago, when he was in a Seattle care facility.

There isn't an ending to this book, our family, or our lives. Just like Charmaine, each of our lives will go forward in the memories that we have had the opportunity to create and share.

Part Three

By Craig Powell

Chapter 1:   I Am Wanted and Loved!

I was born on November 13, 1970. I was adopted by Larry, Gayle, and Charmaine three weeks later.

When I was three months old, my parents heard me scream out while I was in bed. By the time they got to me, I had stopped breathing, and so they rushed me to the hospital while trying to keep me breathing. None of the doctors there could find a definite cause for this episode, but they later said that if I had died, it would have been listed as SIDS.

After I came home, I was different. I didn't like to be touched, and I was awake most days and nights, only sleeping around two hours a day, which drove my mother nuts. When time went on and my sleeplessness continued, she didn't know what to do. One doctor suggested that a little bit of whiskey and a hot bath might make me go to sleep.

My earliest memories are of playing in the yard with Charmaine and Oliver, our dog. When I was four years old, we moved to a new house that was built in a forest. I loved being in the forest for hours and hours. A few months after moving to this house, I got the chicken pox and gave it to my sister. Shortly after that, she got Reye's syndrome and died. I was furious at my mom. I don't know why, but I blamed her for Charmaine's death.

We went to church regularly, but it was kind of weird; I did not know how to fit in. I asked Jesus into my heart. After all, my sister was in heaven, and I wanted to be with her.

I had been acting out ever since I came home from the hospital when I was three months old, but I acted out even more as I grew older. When I was around five years old, I started going to a psychiatrist and a therapist. Around this time, the babysitter was having his way with me, and that made me even angrier.

Chapter 2: Growing Up Too Fast

When I was six years old, we went on vacation and I spent a day with my uncle. He got me to smoke marijuana, and I got stoned out of my mind. I had to lie down in his loft. It was kind of scary, but it was also kind of nice. My parents didn't know about this until I was much older.

School was a struggle for me. I never felt like I fit in. I felt odd, different, and weird. Once when another student teased me, I chased him down, swung him around, and let him go as his head hit the wall. He was admitted to the hospital with a concussion. He was in a coma for three days.

During this time, I was also fighting with my mom—physically chasing her around the house with knives, saying, "Why did you kill my sister? I hate you for this!"

I was in therapy several days a week—sometimes alone and sometimes with my parents. One time I flipped out and ran through the offices, trashing everything in sight. I felt alone and forgotten. I was angry and I missed Charmaine. I wished it had been me who died. Everybody would have been better off anyway.

I went to a hospital in Seattle and was put in the psychiatric ward for six weeks of evaluation. After that I returned to my home and school, and for the next two years I continued to create more trouble for everybody.

Chapter 3:   Moving from Home

Eventually I went back to the same hospital for another six weeks. This time it was recommended that I be put in a residential treatment center. It was a little scary for me there, being only ten years old. There were no doors on our dorm rooms, and there weren't private showers. As one of the smallest kids, I was an easy target for the older boys.

I continued to act out, as did the other kids. The staff would restrain me by pinning me to the ground, putting my arms behind my back, and taking me to my room. If one staff member couldn't handle me, it would take several. Once it took five staff members to get me to my room. I was so disruptive in the classrooms that it was easier for them to put me elsewhere. So at best I got the equivalent of a fifth-grade education. The rest of my growing-up years were without any formal education.

There were times when living at the care facility was fun. We would play basketball and football, and sometimes a few of the Seahawk football players would come and play football with us. I liked playing with them because they were big and strong. I could push and hit them all I wanted and it would not affect them. I even saw one of the players once when I was out to lunch with my parents. This bigger-than-life guy walked up to our table and said, "Hello, Craig." I think he scared my parents. They did not know who he was until he introduced himself. That was a fun day.

But most of the time I did not like living there. It was easy for me to run away, and I did it a lot. One time when I was twelve, I stole a twenty-two-foot sailboat. The Coast Guard finally caught me out in the Puget Sound. They put me in juvenile hall for a while.

Once, upset about how they ran the facility, I barricaded myself and some other kids in our room. I wanted to talk to the governor about our situation. While we were barricaded in, I lost my virginity. After a few days of being closed inside the room, I set a fire, and the staff called the fire department and firefighters broke in. I was still just twelve years old.

Living in group homes and residential treatment centers was kind of lonely. I lost all sense of family life, and visits with my parents were hard, especially around the holidays and birthdays. I didn't feel like I was part of the family most of the time, and I was guarded with new relationships. The staff and caseworkers were trying to figure out what was wrong with me. Doctors were trying hard too, so I knew something was wrong. I knew I wasn't right oftentimes. I still wished I had died instead of Charmaine. Everybody would have been happier.

I was in the first treatment center for almost two years, and then they moved me to a facility on an island in the Puget Sound. I was one of twelve of the worst boys in the country. My first roommate was there for attempted murder. My second roommate was there for armed bank robbery. I was the only one from Washington living on the island. Most of the other boys were older and bigger than I was, and so it was important for me to be tough and let them know I was tough. I remember that one of the boys reached over the table to take something from my dinner plate, and I stuck my fork deep into his hand. This facility had a smoking deck. I learned to smoke when I was twelve.

During a hiking trip on the island, I was on a rope swing that swung way out into the woods, and when I jumped from the swing, somebody was there when I landed on the ground and started hitting me. I fell a long way, shattering my fibula and tibia. One of the staff called for help on the radio. The maintenance man came in an old truck, driving up the dirt roads as far as he could and then hiking the rest of the way. He had always been really nice to me, so I knew he was going to try his hardest to help me.

When he got to me, he said, "You are going to be all right." Knowing it was going to hurt me, he picked me up and carried me, and with every step my leg bounced. It hurt a lot. We finally made it to the truck. He laid me down in the truck bed and then tried to start the truck, but it would not start. So he popped the hood and worked on the engine for about forty minutes. He finally got it to start, and we started down the road to the main building. The tide was out, so they could not get a boat in to pick me up. The maintenance man had to drive to the other side of the bay to get to a radio to call for a boat to pick me up. The staff put me on a stretcher and carried me across the trails and fields to the other building.

When we arrived and they called for a boat, they were told that the water was very rough. Even the ferries were changing course to get through the bay. Fortunately, the facility had a twenty-one-foot Boston Whaler with twin engines.

The trip back to the mainland was so bouncy that it caused my leg to bounce as well. We finally made it back to the dock on the mainland, and I was transported to the hospital in an old van with all the windows broken out. It was unbelievable how everything about this emergency trip had gone wrong.

At the hospital I was greeted by a doctor who told me that my leg was too swollen to be put in a cast. I was given some pain medicine and taken to a hotel for a few days. My caseworkers would come by there to check on me. A few days later, a doctor put on the cast.

Like most group homes, mine had pool tables. I would play pool for five hours a day, and I got to be pretty good. I remember getting into a fight and hitting a kid really hard in the head with a pool cue.

I would also throw pool balls at the staff. Fighting with the staff was a normal thing to do there. The consequence was that you had to sleep in a corner of the room. You also had to dig a ditch, the size of which was determined by how much damage you did. If it was a small fight, you dug a fifty-foot ditch. If it was more serious, like stomping on somebody's head, you had to dig a three-foot-wide, two-foot-deep, hundred-foot-long ditch.

It wasn't all bad. Sometimes you got to play basketball; that I really liked. Playing pool was always fun because I won most of the time. We also got to go on hikes if we were on good behavior.

The one thing all those facilities had in common was that they were temporary homes for me. I always knew I would be moving on to somewhere else, though I was never sure where.

One of the night watchmen introduced me to God, and I prayed and asked Jesus for help in my life. Sometime later I denounced Jesus and asked Satan into my heart. I joined several other boys in drawing upside-down crosses on our chests with markers.

I was on the island for a few years, and then they tried me in a few foster homes, but none of them worked out. They put me in a work group for a while. I forged my own federal ID card while I was there. I was kicked out of work group for selling drugs to other kids. I was sixteen when I shot cocaine into my neck for the first time.

I called my caseworker and was placed in a rehab center in Portland. When my dad came to visit me there, I was a mess. The staff told him that he and my mother should break off all ties with me, that I would probably be dead or in prison within the next six months. Thank God they never gave up on me.

Chapter 4: Eighteen and on My Own

When I turned eighteen, the state released me and I was on my own. My dad set me up in a halfway house in my hometown of Longview and gave me the names of several people to contact for a job. I went through all five jobs within a week. It was a bitch trying to work. My dad had paid for me to be in the halfway house for one month. He also sent one of his employees to me with a hundred dollars. I spent it all on drugs. I ended up living in an abandoned house while I worked ringing the bell at stores during Christmas time. When I got paid, another guy and I would buy cocaine from a local dealer. We eventually ripped off the dealer and had to get out of town before he killed us.

I went to one of my dad's friends and asked for a hundred dollars to get to Seattle. The other guy and I got off the bus there with just the clothes on our back. I did not know where I was going. I was optimistic, though; I was going to make it happen. I just needed to know where to find a shelter. I asked for directions along the way and was pointed to a place like a group home which was surprisingly comfortable, although it was a little dangerous. I was living with a lot of weirdoes.

I found a place where I could get day work if I got there early in the morning. I would wait on a particular corner and chase down pickup trucks. The drivers would want somebody just for the day, to do tough labor.

My second day I was hired to work for a big-time cellular company. They wanted me to help build scaffolding on top of the tallest skyscraper in Seattle. I loved the work, which lasted two days. The view from the top of the skyscraper was magnificent. I made five dollars an hour, enough to pay for my stay at the shelter and buy some cocaine and alcohol. I loved shooting cocaine. It made me feel so good, and it made me feel all right.

Sometimes I would stay out so late getting drugs that the shelter wouldn't let me in, and so I would sleep outside in the alley, where it was very dangerous. I was stupid and young and really didn't know what could happen to me. One night the guy sleeping on the other side of the alley sat straight up and screamed, "Hey, come back with my pants!" It was pretty funny, anyway. It was like that most nights.

I made friends with an older man—he was around forty—who worked for the refineries sometimes. We met while chasing pickup trucks for work. He was addicted to cocaine, and we would get high together. He took me to the refinery where he was working. They did not want to hire me, but he convinced them to give me a chance.

We were staying in small shelter that was something like a cabin. It was so old you could see through walls. It was winter, and pretty cold. When we got our checks, we would buy cocaine and heroin together.

I moved back to Seattle with enough money to rent a small room that included a bathroom and the use of a kitchen that was down the hall, above a store. When I was shown the room, somebody was staying there already, and so I asked how he could rent it to me when somebody was already there. He said that if I wanted it, they would kick out the other person. I found out that this area was primarily African American—it seemed that I was the only white person for blocks—and it was known to have six or seven homicides per year. I figured that if I minded my own business, I would be okay.

I continued to do day labor, chasing pickup trucks to get work. Around that time, I met Sam. We were on a job together doing concrete work. He needed a place to stay, and so I invited him to live with me. He slept on the floor. This is when my addiction started to get really serious. We would work together as day laborers and put our money together to buy cocaine and heroin from a Mexican. His stuff was stronger but cheaper, and I started taking larger and larger amounts. The drugs felt like a freight train going through my head. It was very common for me to fall to my knees and lose my breath. My heart would pound, I would nearly lose consciousness, and I could not feel my body. I would get in the shower and try to shock my system with cool water. I remember collapsing on the floor and trying to stick my head out the window to get my vision back.

Another time I came back to my room and found that Sam had locked me out. I broke in and found him passed out on the floor. His lips were purple and he had peed in his pants. I tried to slap him out of it, and then I dragged him into the shower to shock his system with cold water. He finally came around.

At the time, I was working for a guy named Jim. He seemed to like me, but he couldn't figure out why I lived in the area where I did. After work he would drop me off several blocks from where I was living. He said it was too scary to drive any closer. He offered to help me get off drugs, but I told him I was fine.

Some nights I would go out looking for drugs and wake up in a different part of town. I started missing work, and then I started getting picked up by the police for shoplifting and other petty theft.

I was going downstairs to the store around seven o'clock one night when a bunch of African Americans, probably four or five guys, surrounded me. I knew I was about to get beaten to a pulp.

A friend who lived across the hall from me stuck his head out the window and saw what was happening. The guys surrounding me knew that this man had just been released from a state penitentiary. He was a very large man who lifted weights a lot. I had seen this gang beat up other guys by kicking victims in the back and stomping on their heads. But when this gang realized that my friend was coming down to protect me, they left me alone. I went on to the store without any other problems. I thanked God for looking after me.

When I went back to work a few days later, I was still really high from the night before, when I'd smoked pot, drunk cocaine and heroin, and then dropped a couple of hits of acid. I was supposed to be painting a large house with a ten-car garage, but I set my paintbrush down for a few minutes and then couldn't find it again. I knocked on the door and told Dave that I wanted him to help me get off drugs.

Dave did not want me going back to the room I was renting; he wanted me to find a safer place to live. But it was a busy weekend in Seattle, and we could not find another place for me to stay. I ended up living with him, sleeping on his couch. Dave was newly engaged, and his fiancée had two young daughters who were probably eighteen and twenty years old. I could not believe he would let me live in the house with them. I felt like family.

So I lived at Dave's house and worked for him, painting his house and boat plus another house. This went on for a while, but I continued to drink. We kept looking for a place for me to live but didn't find anything that I could get into, so he cosigned a lease so I could get a nice apartment. I would just pay him monthly. Piece by piece, I bought some used furniture.

One night I invited Dave and his wife over for dinner. I made them spaghetti. By then I had a full-time job building foundations, and Dave asked me if I wanted an easier job inside, where it was warm and dry. He introduced me to one of his business partners.

The man owned a vending company, and Dave told him that I would be a great driver and deliveryman. The partner was hesitant; he asked me to leave the room. I think Dave reminded him that he would be nothing without Dave's investments. Anyone could have done the job, and so I did it for a couple of months, driving a hundred miles each day. Meanwhile Dave would invite me over to his house, mostly on weekends, to watch basketball or football or just hang out and have something to eat and drink with his family.

I ran into one of my old friends from the island facility. He said he needed a place to stay for three weeks, and after that he was going to Alaska to work on a fishing boat. He would be back in two months with $10,000. I did not believe him until he came back in two months with $10,000. We partied hard, he was very thankful that I'd given him a place to stay for a while. When he asked me to join him on the next fishing trip, I agreed, and we partied every night with some girls until we left for Alaska.

Eventually I worked my way back to the drugs. Needing a place where I could stay warm and be able to sleep, I would go to the Seattle airport and dig through the trash to find a used ticket. Then I would sleep in the waiting area. I also would sleep in the train station or in a multilevel parking lot.

As I got weaker and my body started breaking down, I stopped working to pay for my drugs. I started lying, stealing, and scamming just to get more drugs to put into my body. I felt worthless, and so pissed off at myself. I loved heroin. It was like a big hug; it made me feel warm all over. The drugs would help me forget everything.

One day I ran into this guy and we ended up getting a bunch of drugs and going to his house, where we got really, really high shooting cocaine. The next thing I knew, I heard glass breaking and the wall had a hole in it and then there was more glass breaking. I'd experienced my first drive-by shooting. About ten minutes later, the apartment was filled with police. I was completely high and out of my mind. The police couldn't have cared less about our condition or our drugs. They left to look for the people who had done the shooting.

Another night, I hooked up with a guy and we went to get drugs, and I was so high that I dropped the drugs out of the moving car. He stopped the car and told me to get out and try to find them. When I did, he took them from me and started to drive off. I grabbed the car, and he dragged me for about three blocks. He eventually stopped, but when I walked behind the car, he backed over me. He left me standing in the middle of the street at 3:00 a.m. with both legs bleeding. I really don't remember anything after that.

Chapter 5:   My First Christmas as an Adult

That December I called my parents, and they invited me to come to their house for Christmas. My dad arranged for me to take the bus to Portland. I quit heroin, cocaine, and cigarettes before leaving Seattle. My parents did not like smoke in their house. By Christmas Eve I was shaking and sweating, and my mom and dad were very concerned. Dad took me to the emergency room, where the doctor said that I was going through withdrawals and there was nothing he could do. The next day my dad put me on a plane back to Seattle, giving me some money for a taxi when I got there. I took the gifts they'd given me for Christmas and sold them at the Portland airport before my flight.

On the flight, I sat next to a lady who told me about Jesus. I tried to be as polite as I could be; I did not have much fight left in me from the withdrawals. I ignored her when she told me that Jesus loved me.

When I got off the plane, I went straight to my dealer for more drugs. I knew they were not good for me, but I could not stop. I thought about jumping off an overpass into traffic, but I was too strung out.

The first time I tried to kill myself, I was twelve years old. I attempted to hang myself in the closet in a group home. Another time I grabbed a bunch of drugs from a guard's hand and swallowed them, but they took me to the hospital to have my stomach pumped.

I continued doing more and more dangerous things with dangerous people. I knew my time was short. I would call my dad often for short periods of time, and then I would not call him for months. I started calling him again every week for several weeks, each time telling him that it was probably going to be the last time we talked. I was always high, so I don't remember his reaction.

At this point I was on the streets, and I'd watch people going to work early in the morning. They would always walk way around me, and they never made eye contact. I would go to one of the stadiums and watch families come out after the game. I wanted to be part of a family too, but drugs kept getting in the way.

After I ripped off some people at knifepoint, the police began looking for me. I left for Everett, finally feeling that it was time to change my life and ask for some help. I had been in and out of several shelters and had heard the words of God. They had not affected me at the time, but now I was ready. I went to the front desk of a shelter and asked for help. The desk attendant sent me away because I was high, telling me to sober up and come back another time. I was going through withdrawals, and the only place I could find shelter was under the freeway overpass. It was January, and the temperature was in the teens. I did the rest of my drugs.

When I was somewhat sober, I went back to the mission and asked for the chaplain, a guy named Tom. He said I would need to go through detox before I could stay there, and he offered to call for the detox van. I agreed and the van came to pick me up. When I got in the van, I started to cry. I hadn't cried in years. I was just so broken down that I could not control myself. I was asking God for deliverance and help to change my life.

This was not my first time going to detox, but it was the first time I really wanted to quit drugs. In the past it had just been a nice break to give my body a rest, take a shower, eat some food, and sleep indoors in a real bed. The people there really seemed to care more than the staff at other places. Most of the other shelters had a discipleship program where they would mentor you and teach you about God and encourage you to have a relationship with him.

I joined the mission's program, but it was really hard. I was bouncing off the walls, and I was sick a lot. It had been so long since I had been straight that I didn't know who I was; I didn't know how to act or react. One minute I would be happy, and the next I would be in somebody's face, yelling and screaming and threatening him. My mood was up and down for more than a week.

Tom and I gradually became friends. He was the only person I could talk to about my life—not like the chaplains at some of the other places I'd been. I was a corner-to-corner junkie, and my heart was black. I hated people.

I stayed there for a while, and I started to level out after about six months to a year. In the beginning, it was even hard for me to speak in complete sentences that made any sense. I was pretty scared, but I had hope in a new relationship with Jesus. I knew it was real; I could feel it inside me, like some sort of an awakening. Up until then I'd thought it was all bs.

Chapter 6:   I Am Still Alive

I started calling my parents again. They were relieved that I was still alive and was getting some help. I was in a good place, and on Sundays I started going to the same church that Tom went to. I met his daughter there a couple of times, and he introduced me to some church members who would give me jobs working on pole buildings. I had a small group of friends in the church, mostly older people who were reaching out to me. They were very tolerant; looking back, I don't know how they put up with me.

I ended up staying with some people, renting a room in their house for a while. I would also visit Tom at his house; we would sit on his couch and watch boxing on Tuesdays and Fridays. He offered to let me stay and sleep on his couch one night, and then the arrangement became more long-term, so I moved outside into his chicken coop. I cleaned it up and bought a wood stove and a bed.

I was working in Seattle and living in Everett. At nights when I came home, I would spend time talking to his daughter, who was about ten years younger than I was. We would go for walks, and soon we became close.

Eventually I needed to find a different place to live, and so I rented an apartment (really a converted garage) from some people I knew from church. It was a few miles from where Tom's daughter lived, and she would come over to visit me sometimes. She was very sheltered, and I was the complete opposite. I knew nothing about dating or anything like that, but she gave me positive attention that made me feel good about myself.

Chapter 7:   Marriage and Family

We eventually got married. My parents came to the wedding and hosted a rehearsal dinner for about twenty-five people. I was nervous before the wedding, but my parents and I spent some time out in front of the church, talking and laughing a lot about nothing in particular. For our honeymoon, my parents rented us a house, a bed and breakfast on an island in the Puget Sound. It was really nice, and we appreciated the gesture.

I started my own painting business, and it was very successful. Within a year of our marriage, we bought a house. Then we bought another house located downtown, to use as a rental.

When our son was about to be born, I was so excited. This was my first and only child, so all I really knew about childbirth was what I'd seen on TV. I drove to the hospital really fast and got my wife into her room at the hospital. She was uncomfortable, and I was saying things like, "It's going to be all right."

She was dilating and things seemed to be moving along when the doctor came in and noticed that there were some serious complications with our son's heartbeat. I didn't really understand what was going on, but I could see that people were really concerned. It sounded like they didn't have a plan. They pulled me out of the room and told me that there was poop or something in the amniotic fluid, and that it could have a real negative effect on my son. This was a serious concern, and I was trying to figure out what was going on. When I asked about his chances of survival, they said maybe fifty-fifty; they didn't know if he was going to make it.

While they brought in a specialist from another hospital, I called my dad and tried to explain what was going on. He and my mom were driving to the hospital from Portland, but they were still a few hours away. I tried to tell him that maybe they should turn around and go home. They said that they would not go back and they would be there as soon as possible.

I went back into the room with my wife and told her she was doing great. I told her that there weren't any problems, that the doctors were just being safe. She had enough to deal with, so there was no point in making her worry. I was a complete wreck, although by then the doctor from the other hospital was there. I tried to hide my emotions when they came to take my wife into delivery. Logan was ready to come into this world.

This delivery did not look like the ones I had seen on television. When they pulled the baby out, he was gray. The doctors tried to get him to breathe by slapping his butt, and all of a sudden he was breathing. I couldn't believe it. A second later, they took him off to the ICU. The doctors were amazing, but they still were not sure if he was going to make it.

My wife kept asking where her baby was, and I told her that they were doing some routine tests. She finally fell asleep, and I went to the ICU to check on my son. As I was looking at him through the window, he lifted his head up. The nurses said that it was a big deal for him to do that. I said, "Of course. He is my son."

When my mom and dad showed up, I explained what had gone on. By then the baby was stable and his mother was sleeping.

My parents went to my house, and my mom jumped into action in the kitchen, taking a full inventory of what we had and what we needed for the baby and his mom. Dad then went to the store and got the necessities Mom had asked for. Watching my mom and dad come in and help like that, looking out for my family and me, was really overwhelming and new.

My wife and I didn't do very well together, and we really didn't have anything in common. She would stay home while I went to church. I was part of a men's prayer group that met on Wednesday nights. I was also a Sunday school teacher. I tried to get her to come and join me in teaching the kids, but she wasn't interested. Advice from church members didn't help at all; we were too far apart. She was hanging out with one of my employees, the guy who was renting my house downtown. She eventually took our son and moved in with him, saying she wanted to end our marriage. It was an ugly divorce that took a long time to settle.

Chapter 8:   It Starts All Over

I started drinking again, and then soon after that I was using drugs again. I was depressed, and I felt like a failure for letting my son down. I really loved him, but I did not want him to see me in that kind of shape. I had thought I was doing everything right.

Now I was shunned at church. I'd spent a lot of quality time with these people—we all helped build the church, and we all would sing to Jesus—but when things got tough, it was like a ghost town. There was one guy in the church who still seemed to care about me; he was not part of the main clique. He came over to my house one day to check on me, and I was embarrassed that I was in such bad shape. I was very thin and looked like hell. The bank had just completed a quick sell my houses. I'd hidden large amounts of heroin in my main house, and for about a year I'd just sat on the couch, shooting heroin. I finally had to move to my other house downtown.

When I arrived at that house, the power and water had been turned off and the house was a mess. It was in the process of being repossessed.

I had given up. I was completely depleted, and I didn't have any veins that I could shoot up with heroin. I had abscesses all over my body. I couldn't even see or play with my son. By then he was three, and it was best for him not to see me like that. He was the sweetest little boy and did not deserve that. I loved him so much, but I did not have anything left to give him.

When I was getting food from a man at the food bank, he began talking to me about God. He was easy to talk to. There was another guy who lived two doors down from me, and he also would talk about God. He was from South Central LA and had a serious drug problem; he went to this outreach place in Los Angeles. He told me that there was a place like it in Seattle, and that if I wanted help I could come see him. I told him that I was fine, that I didn't need anybody's help.

I continued to sell things from my house and get high. Finally, I ended up sleeping on couch cushions on the floor—that's all that was left—with only candles for light.

One night I heard somebody wiggling the doorknob. It was some people I had ripped off before. I tried to keep the door closed, but one of the guys pushed the door in. We struggled and he got the best of me. His friend walked in behind him wearing rain gear and holding a large automatic rifle. He pointed it at my head. I was on my knees. The other guy was looking for a tarp. I knew this was the end of my life. My life flashed before my eyes, and I remember seeing flashes of my son. I said out loud, "Forgive me, as I have sinned in the name of Jesus Christ." I prayed that I would go to heaven, knowing that I needed to profess it out loud.

They just beat me up and stole my vehicle, leaving me terrified. I waited until morning and then went to find my friend.

I was dope sick and freaked out and needed help. He made some phone calls and drove me to a church in downtown Seattle. I went into the church throwing up all over the place, and this woman walked up to me, gave me a hug, and said, "Welcome home. You're in the right place." Then she gave me a kiss on the cheek and asked me to sit down wherever I wanted.

I sat in the back of the church, throwing up into a trash can. The preacher came over and looked at me; he wanted me to go with some other guys to the hospital. I said that I needed food and rest, and so they took me to a small house that I would be sharing with ten or twelve guys. We each had a bunk bed—that was all the furniture in the house—and there was one bathroom. It was pretty ghetto, but I was glad to be there.

I was watching them make some food that they were planning to give me, when I blew chunks all over the kitchen. I went to bed and stayed there for eight or nine days. They would bring me food, and I started to feel better. I had to get up with them at five o'clock in the morning to attend prayers on our hands and knees in a classroom. I remember that I had hardly the strength to walk there.

A month or two later, my realtor, who was handling a quick sale of my house, found me. He would visit me on occasion to have me sign paperwork.

Shortly after that, I ended up at a different shelter. At the time I was six-feet-one and weighed 135 pounds. I was incredibly weak, and my spirit was broken. I was at the all-time bottom of my failing life. This new shelter did not have room for me, so they put me on a bed in the hallway. I remember lying there for hours, staring at a picture of Jesus walking on water, and that somehow gave me hope.

Some of the people staying there would walk by me and say crazy things. I was really sick; as it turned out, I had five abscesses. They finally sent me to the hospital. The abscesses were pretty severe. I had them on my arms and shoulders and on my groin area. I stayed in the hospital for a week, but it took six weeks to completely heal.

When I was in the shelter, I experienced a very real and new relationship with God. I stayed clean for almost a year. I talked to the chaplain at the shelter, and he said it was time to take care of my warrants. I wasn't scared anymore; I just wanted to do the next right thing. I was at peace about it. So I turned myself in at the police and stayed in jail until I was processed to a minimum-security location. While I was waiting for sentencing, a friend of mine who had similar charges—actually one less charge and fewer priors than I had—went in for sentencing and received two and a half years. So I knew I was going to go to prison, no doubt about it.

I called my parents and let them know that I was going to go away for a while, and that I would call them when I got out of jail. I wasn't praying not to have to go to jail, or anything like that. I was fine with whatever the outcome was going to be.

Later that week, I was transported to the jail at the courthouse. It was 9:10 p.m. by the time I saw the judge. He listened to the case, but I didn't have any defense; I was guilty. And then out of the blue, the weirdest thing happened: the judge released me. I couldn't believe it. He said I could go free.

I hadn't planned for that. Then I proceeded to tell him that there were outstanding warrants for my arrest in the computer system. I said, "Please double-check, because they will double-check my record when they get ready to release me at the end of processing." I did not want to go through the whole release process knowing that they were just going to turn around and put me back in jail.

The judge checked over my record and gave me the green light. I still couldn't believe it when they released me six or seven hours later. There I was, free on the streets of downtown Seattle.

The first thing I did was go searching for drugs.

I found some heroin and a needle, and the next thing I knew I was in an alley, being awakened by the police. I'd been sleeping on a roll of carpet, and they told me that I could not sleep there. When I finally got to my feet, I was a mess. I couldn't believe that after everything God had done for me, I had gone out and gotten loaded. What a slap in the face of God.

Chapter 9:   Touched by an Angel

I was walking down the streets of Seattle at six thirty in the morning, crying out to God for help. Why would God even listen to me at that point after I'd just gotten high again? I started feeling sick from withdrawal. My body was full of pain, and I felt lousy, like I was going to puke. I went into a bar that had ten or fifteen people inside, and I noticed this gentleman walking around, asking people about someone he was looking for. He eventually walked up to me and asked me if I knew this person and if could I help find him. We talked awhile, and he told me that he had looked all over the Seattle area for this man and thought he may have moved to Bellingham. Then he asked if I would go with him to help find the man.

I had wanted to go to Bellingham for some time, because it was a little more laid back and did not have such a wide availability of drugs. It was very difficult for me to get out of Seattle, but if I left it would be very hard for me to find the drugs I wanted. I decided this might be my best chance to get to a new life and break away from drugs.

This individual asking me to go to Bellingham to look for his friend was like divine intervention. I told him that I would go to Bellingham with him as long as he would drop me off in Everett on the way back.

As we were walking out the door of the bar—it exited out onto an alley—I asked him if he knew the Lord. He replied, "You have no idea. You are in good hands."

When we got into his car and started our travels, I was a wreck mentally and emotionally, and my body ached all over. As we traveled down the freeway, we talked for a while, and then I started crying. At first things felt really weird, but then the guy began telling me stories about how he was in prison when God came into his life, and what prison was really like. I commented that God was really powerful, and he said, "You haven't seen the tip of the iceberg."

As we drove down a long hill and into a lowland area, and he reached over and put his hand on my knee. He said, "When we go into this valley, God is going to take all your pain away."

I thought he'd lost his mind. But sure enough, we went down that hill and the pain and mental stress were gone. I was full of joy. I have heard people say, "God helps those who help themselves." I think that's a load of crap. I think God helps those who can't help themselves.

By this time, I was wondering, *Who is this guy?* I asked him his name, and he said, "You know, God has sent me on these missions before, and when I tell people my name, it ruins it for them. All you need to know is that God sent me to look out for you."

We got to Bellingham and looked for his friend but could not find him, and so we turned back, heading toward Everett. On the way, he told me that God had a huge plan for my life, one well beyond my comprehension. As I sat there, I wondered what God's plan was.

We pulled up to my stop and he let me out of the car. I grabbed my bag and got out, and he drove off. At that point all the pain returned to my body. I did make it back to the shelter.

I finally started communicating with my parents again. They said they'd been concerned about me and were glad to hear that I was getting better. Still, I was at an all-time low: I had lost my son, three houses, and my business. I did not know if I could come back this time. I had already worked my way off the streets of Seattle once, and I didn't know if I could do it again. I kept reaching out to God, and he renewed my strength little by little.

Chapter 10: A Helping Hand

I talked to my dad about the details involved in starting over, and he said the family would help me. He and Mom asked me to come to their house and paint the interior for them. They would buy all the necessary tools plus pay the going rate for the work I was going to do. Dad then talked his brother into providing enough money for me to get licensed, bonded, and insured and retain my contractor's license, and my cousin lent me money to buy a used van. I couldn't believe they were all there for me. I didn't want to let them down.

I was still in the recovery process. My mind was really muddled, and it was hard to construct sentences and thoughts. But I bought a van and went to work for a friend who owned a large company, just to get my feet on the ground. I was paying child support, but my divorce had not been finalized yet; the attorneys were still arguing over money. It was kind of funny: I don't think they realized I was still living in a shelter. One time they sent a guy to come collect from me at the shelter; he wanted me to pay $3,900 a month. He was very aggressive. A friend of mine who had just gotten out of jail got in between the collector and me and showed him the door.

I had a van that ran, kind of—black smoke came out of the back, and I was not a mechanic. I was trying to work while constantly going to court over the divorce and taking court-imposed parenting classes, and all the judge could say was, "Where is the money?" My wife had left me for one of my employees and taken my son with her. The courts really looked down on fathers, even in this situation, when there had been some domestic violence at the house and the mother had gone to jail. I had done a lot of screwing up myself, so obviously I wasn't a great pick for a custodial parent either. I was determined to get my son back somehow. I was going to make some changes, and I was not going to fail him—even after the many ups and downs of being evicted from various apartments, being in and out of psych wards, and having my car break down. Everything that could go wrong had gone wrong.

I moved to Bellingham, where my son lived. I figured I could be broke and start over anywhere; I might as well be in the same town as my son.

Back when I was in Seattle and my son came down to visit me, I took him to Alki Beach and taught him how to ride the bike that I had gotten for him. I put a helmet on him and told him to ride in every mud puddle he could see. He proceeded to do so with a big smile on his face. "Look, Dad, I am doing it!" he would shout. He was the sweetest kid ever. He was the only good thing in my life. I loved him so much. But I'd struggled while he was at his mom's. I took his bike and pawned it so I could put more drugs in my arm.

When I moved to Bellingham, I had an old, beat-up van, half a pack of cigarettes, some toys for my son, and the clothes on my back. I had no money, no gas, and no real understanding of how to get around the town. I knew my son lived there, though, and I was going to start over and be a part of his life, no matter what.

I was on my second day at a new job when I met a woman. Two weeks later, we became friends, and then we became lovers. I was visiting my son on a regular basis, just for day visits. I had nowhere to take him, but I was on the straight and narrow. I was just drinking every day and doing a little bit of cocaine now and again. For me, that was pretty much sober. Going to work and having a few beers with this woman was a normal day.

Then my drinking got a little out of hand. One night I lost control and ended up in a fight in a back lot of a pub. I did not get hurt, but the other guy did. My girlfriend got mad and said that I had a problem. I replied that the problem was that I'd kicked the guy's tail. She said that she hadn't signed up for that, and that she had a couple of kids and was looking for more than what I had to offer. If I wanted to stay around and be part of a family, she said, I needed to get help.

I started going to a twelve-step program.

Chapter 11: A Program That Saved My Life

The meetings did not make much sense to me, but going to them kept me in good standing with this woman. As I was completely insecure and longing for affection and intimacy, I went, saying they were a big help. But for me it was all about the rescue sex.

That is how I got my first ten months of sobriety. One way or the other, it worked and I was better for it. While I was in the process of getting sober and trying to put my life together, she was helping me with the paperwork for my outstanding debts. However, we didn't have any money, and she had two daughters and a son. The girls lived with us, and the son shared his time between his mom's and dad's houses. Then she took some out-of-state work for more pay and my business started to pick up.

We got married on our deck on the lake where we lived. It was just us, the pastor, and her kids. I called my parents from the end of the dock and told them I'd gotten married.

Then I found out that this woman was sleeping with somebody else. It was close to the end of the month, when all my bills were due. I called my dad—not to ask for money, but to get his advice. I knew he had had a difficult time once and worked his way out of it. To my surprise, a couple of days later I received enough money to pay my bills. I called him back and thanked him, promising I would pay him back. He said not to worry about it, that I had helped him out before.

I was still trying to work things out with my second wife when I started going to a different twelve-step program and met a guy named Don, who would become my sponsor. What a sponsor does is help you identify your character defects and challenges, plus introduce you to a spiritual solution to your problems. It is hard to find a good sponsor, and usually a person who needs a sponsor asks somebody to sponsor him without really knowing what he's asking for. In my case, again, there was divine intervention. I was not all in at the time, and I had thought of asking another man for help, but I stuck with Don. I thought the whole thing was ridiculous and humorous, but I wasn't the first clown Don had dealt with. In fact, we became close friends.

Don definitely knew what he was talking about. The thing that was different with him was that he had a God solution. We didn't necessarily have the same God, but it didn't matter. He didn't care if he pointed me toward my God or his. He was amazing. Up to that point, I only knew how to react to a problem or something that pissed me off, and I would react in anger. That was all I knew: how to react. If I was driving and traffic was slow, I would get mad. I would get mad even waiting in line in the store. Any time someone wasn't thinking about me first, I was offended. And I was always right—nobody could tell me different.

However, Don stood about a foot taller than me and had a no-bull background. He would start saying crazy things, like I was self-centered, inconsiderate, and selfish. At first I was offended by these statements. I would say, "Don't you know what happened to me?" and he would say, "Oh, now you are going to play the victim? Are you going to blame everybody else for your life?" I told him that the one thing he could count on was that I would not take responsibility for my actions. He said it was time for me to grow up or go back to my old ways and die.

He was right, and while I was going to meetings, paying child support, and not getting loaded, I started feeling better emotionally, mentally, and spiritually. He insisted that I help others; I hated that, and I fought him the whole way. He wanted me to help out at meetings, doing things like making the coffee and setting up chairs, and to help people move when they needed a hand. The funny part about it is that I was happy to help others out, and Don was quick to point that out. He explained that if you want to be happy, you have to ask yourself, *What would God have me do today?* I thought, *Who is this guy? He doesn't even go to church.* But Don was right. He said, "God gave you this platform, this opportunity to get sober and to have a good life, and all he wants from you, Craig, is to help your son."

At the time I was hurting so badly in my gut that I felt like I was tied to a tree and someone was carving the flesh from my body. I was at odds with everybody: my ex-wife, the courts, my parents, and myself. In my mind, all the bad stuff had happened to me; it wasn't my fault. Poor Craig. Don showed me that I had been a part of everything, that there were other people on this planet besides me, and that they had thoughts and feelings. I had never thought about that before. I'd never thought about what life was like for my parents or my son or even my ex-wife. I could only think about me.

One of the twelve steps is to take a fearless moral inventory of yourself. I was scared to do that, but I'd been getting better up to that point and I couldn't stop now. Some people say they feel great after they do the fourth step; they have a breakthrough. I was embarrassed that I had acted like a victim all my life and blamed everybody else for my problems. Deep down, I wanted to be a great dad. How could I have been such a wimp?

I called Don a couple of days later and said, "I don't think this is working. I feel crappier now than I ever did."

As usual, he said something spiritual and added, "We're going to act better than we feel today." He told me that spirituality isn't a feeling, but an action. You say and choose the actions you're going to take. If you want to keep doing what you do, you keep getting what you got. Or you can do something new and different to change the situation. That's where the rubber meets the road.

I had maybe a year and a half clean. I'd never had this much time before, and I actually had friends, not just people waiting for the opportunity to take advantage of me. Don helped me with every decision and direction. I was moving forward, and we would talk about my direction. He would point out what I really wanted and how to get there in my relationship with God, my relationships with people, and in my business. Up until then, all my relationships had been disasters. This was a complete mental overhaul, and in the end I found out that I was just a scared little boy who'd never grown up. I blamed my problems on everybody else, including God. Don helped me see what I really wanted to be: a regular guy who was comfortable in his own skin, and a loving, supportive dad and a loving, caring son. Going through life without being in constant conflict with others was a real revelation.

Chapter 12: It's Time to Live

I was at a point in my life when I had consistent visitation with my son. I was starting to grow spiritually. I had realized how dysfunctional my second marriage was and decided to call it quits.

This was the best I'd felt in my entire life. I was free, and I knew what to do. Every day I would ask God, *What would you have me do today?* His answer was to help others, provide for my son, and go to meetings, plus keep up my relationship with Don.

My son was up and down emotionally; he was insecure and had no confidence. I felt that he needed more time with me so I could help build him up from within. I was scared for him.

Don told me that my ex-wife was one of God's children and so I should help her. Even though I thought it was crazy, I did try by helping her take care of our son. He started staying at my house more and more weekends, and that eventually turned into months. Each day I would drive him to and from school, an hour each way. This went on for most of the school year. He was happy, and he felt safe and secure. He was protected and provided for on a daily basis. I continued to pay child support even though he was staying with me most of the time. I didn't care; it was important for him, and that is what mattered. If I didn't continue to pay it, he would have to go back with her. I really didn't have any choice. She was free to take him any time she wanted, however, and that really bothered me. I couldn't sleep at night, and I cried. I was scared for my son.

He started making friends in my neighborhood, and I became friends with his friends' parents. One family invited us for a weekend trip on their boat to one of the islands. This was one of the nicest things that happened to us. His friend's mother wanted me to meet one of her friends, and so the family invited us to their house for a Fourth of July celebration. There was several guests including this beautiful young woman. I didn't really talk to her; I was speechless and definitely nervous.

A little while later, the family invited me on a boat ride out to the island, and guess who was on the boat? That same beautify young woman. I think somebody was trying to set us up. We had a great time, and a relationship started to develop—slowly, painfully slowly. She was not one to jump into anything very quickly, although I wore her down over time. For sure I would never have given up or quit on her.

My son was back with his mom for the summer, but I suggested that he could stay with me and go to school in my district next year, and she could see him any time she wanted. She said, "No way," and started talking about going in a different direction. However, a month or two went by, and at the last minute before school started, she decided that it would be in his best interest to go to school in my school district and stay with me. He stayed for about five months, and then his mother threatened to come by and take him. I could not sleep. I was terrified for him but scared to do anything about it.

How could a guy like me get custody of his son in this state? They don't like single dads up here. I called Don, and he pointed out that I needed to take the right action and trust God for the results. I was terrified that I would lose custody. How could I win, anyway? I spoke to a couple of lawyers to see what my chances were. I found out that a custody battle would be expensive, and I told the lawyer to wait while I called somebody. I called Don and we talked it over, and I came to the conclusion that my son needed me more than ever. I would not back down.

The lawyer had the venue switched to Bellingham. That gave us home court advantage.

Things were up in the air for a few months. When my ex-wife called me and said there was no way I was going to win, I told her, "I'm not trying to win. I just want our son to win." I also told her that it wasn't about me, and that in the end I wanted full custody. My son had a home; he knew where he lived now, and he felt safe. I couldn't believe how my whole life had changed. I finally had the opportunity to be the father he needed.

I still had work to do as far as the twelve steps went. It was time for me to follow through with the ninth step and make amends. At the top of my list of people to make amends with were my mom and dad. I didn't know how to do it; I was terrified. I talked to my sponsor, Don, who said he was going to Portland for a twelve-step presentation. He asked me to ride with him, suggesting that we could go to my parents' house together.

I prepared myself to point out my wrong actions and acknowledge how they had hurt my mom and dad. I would do it without excuses or justifications or "buts." This was about actions I'd taken and how I had harmed people who were close to me. I would need to understand their feelings about my actions and to recognize my bad behavior and not repeat it.

There were a lot of tears that day. I asked my parents, "Is there anything I left out?"

My mom looked at my dad and said, "Should we tell him, Larry?"

My dad said, "Sure. It is time to let him know some of what we went through."

He said that several years earlier, a hospital staffer had called them to say that I'd been found dead in a public bathroom with a needle stuck in my neck. The staff brought me back to life three different times that day. This call was very emotional for them.

They had already watched their daughter die, and it was looking like it would be the same with their son. Ultimately I was saved, but the hospital never called my parents back to tell them that I was still alive. It was months before they heard from the mission where I was taken after I was released from the hospital.

I could not imagine how my parents had felt during this time, and I had no recollection of the event itself. This was the life I lived for many years, and I am sure it affected them a great deal.

I explained to my parents that I had marinated in victim sauce for decades and had been completely self-consumed. I'd also had no regard for them as people, not to mention as my parents, during that time.

When we finished, we all stood up and hugged and said how much we loved each other. After leaving my parents at their home, Don and I headed to Portland for his presentation. He told me that I was fortunate to have such extraordinary parents. "Those were the most amazing people I've ever met," he said. "You're lucky to have them in your life."

I looked at him and said, "Yeah, but I died. Did you pick up on that?"

This time with my parents and Don, there was a breakthrough. Now we have the opportunity for a new beginning.

There is not an ending to our story, as we continue to grow closer to one another. We have truly been blessed by God, and we look forward to what is yet to come our way. May God bless each of you as he has blessed our family.

About the Authors

Larry and Gayle Powell have been married more than fifty years. Their daughter, Charmaine, died at age eight.

Craig Powell, Larry and Gayle's son, is now a father and business owner.

Contact us

www.authorsthreellc.com

Printed in the United States
By Bookmasters